One More
MILE

James Collins

Published by

 GENERAL STORE
GSPH PUBLISHING HOUSE

499 O'Brien Road, Box 415
Renfrew, Ontario, Canada K7V 4A6
Telephone (613) 432-7697 or 1-800-465-6072

ISBN 1-897113-01-3
Printed and bound in Canada

Cover design and layout by Custom Printers
Cover Photo: Jim Collins
Author Photo: Ginger Collins

General Store Publishing House
Renfrew, Ontario, Canada

Library and Archives Canada Cataloguing in Publication

Collins, James, 1949-
   One man's mile / James Collins ; Jane Karchmar, editor.

ISBN 1-897113-01-3

   1. Collins, James, 1949- 2. Anglican Church of Canada—Clergy—
Biography. 3. Cree Indians—Ontario—Moose Factory Island.
I. Karchmar, Jane II. Title.

BX5620.C62A3 2004   283'.092   C2004-904792-2

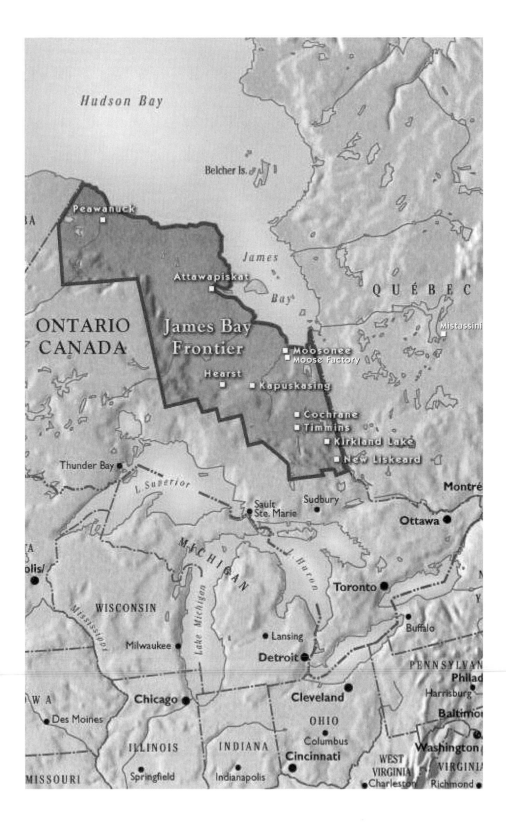

Lorna:

I hope you enjoy
Rio.

11/7/12

Contents

Introduction

I experienced two different worlds growing up in a middle-class, suburban neighbourhood. I walked to school in my button-down-collared shirt, carrying, under my arm, books neatly bound with brown dust covers. At home, my parents supervised my chores. They watched as I went off to school, secure in the education I was receiving.

I lived another life, every summer, vacationing at a rustic cabin on a lake in Southern Ontario. Whether exploring the lake in a flat-bottomed rowboat propelled by an ancient two-and-a-half horsepower outboard motor, or hiking in the woods, my love for the outdoors was nurtured by everything I saw, felt, and smelled. I learned to navigate on the lake by identifying landmarks on the horizon when darkness hid the features of the shoreline except for the highest silhouettes. At first, I learned to walk through the deep woods orienting myself to the sun, or a ridge of land, a lake, or a creek. Later, a compass became my constant companion. I dreamed of living in the woods.

In the pristine vastness of Northern Ontario and Quebec, the Crees exist in two worlds. They live as their ancestors have done for thousands of years, hunting and trapping. Cree parents still pass traditional skills on to their children to preserve a precious way of life. Yet they also live in the modern world of cities and video games. Parents watch as their children go off to school, learning to function in a world which, although right next door, is foreign and often contradictory to their traditional values.

My boyhood fantasy of a life in the woods became reality when, as a young seminary graduate, I travelled with my wife from Boston to Northern Ontario as the new curate at St. Thomas Church, Moose Factory Island. Armed with a Masters of Divinity degree, I was prepared to answer questions that no one was asking. Although neither my professors nor I suspected it, my theological education and accompanying life experience were relevant to only a fraction of the world's population.

I found that I was a tradesman without tools when I arrived at my post. I could not speak to anyone in the village over thirty years of age. I did not understand the circumstances of village life. I was unaware of social customs. Even church life was far different from my training. I studied the Cree language, several hours daily, under the tutelage of my mentor, the parish priest, himself a Cree. I studied the dialect in which the Bible and prayer book had been translated a century before, now spoken only on Moose Factory Island. Diocesan officials did not realize this. There was a bright side to this oversight. As I travelled across the North, the fact that I spoke the same dialect in which the Bible was written lent authority to my words no matter how badly my linguistic ineptitude garbled the message.

I could not help initially experiencing each new encounter with the native people from ingrained cultural presuppositions. A sense of humour helped me live from day to day, circumstance to circumstance, learning and growing, while laughing at how my world fit like a square peg into the round hole of native life.

Dozens of simple life events, complicated by misunderstanding and preconception, became moments for laughter and learning across cultural and linguistic boundaries. Some are related in this book. Each incident described has been rattling around in my memory for almost thirty years, reminding me of youthful zeal, and of those subject to its indiscretions who showed love and forbearance while attempting to discern a message offered in a way more appropriate to another place.

Names may be remembered inaccurately, and conversations may be paraphrased, but the impact of two cultural outlooks on everyday circumstances in the midst of the power and beauty of the created order is accurate. Nowhere, in this age of instant messages and electronic mail, where wars are broadcast live, and natural disasters brought to homes thousands of miles from where they occur, can humanity avoid interaction with different representatives of the species. This demands tolerance, understanding, and a willingness to laugh when personal life imperatives become silly or irrelevant.

I am still astounded by the insights into life gained while working and playing, hunting and camping, with the Crees. The stories in this small collection were experienced, over more than a quarter century, with a people living an ancient life in a modern world.

The Mittens

The morning was crisp and clear. Moisture hung in the air, frozen like millions of little diamonds. Smoke from morning fires rose in straight, grey lines to bend and congeal into a soft layer of haze diffusing the light. Although it was mid-morning, time seemed suspended with the lack of human activity and the dream-like quality of the elements around me.

I felt all the signs of extreme cold. I knew the temperature within a few degrees, even without my morning glance at the thermometer. My nostrils were frozen. My eyelids were heavy with frost from my breath. The snow crunched under my feet, spreading like moon dust with every step. I had a long way to walk, but I was enjoying the frozen solitude. My outer clothing formed a cocoon that afforded a delicious feeling of warmth in the frigid air. A heavy hooded parka held in my body heat. The hood was pulled up and tightly tied. Wolf fur, white with breath frost, ringed my face. My feet were warm balls in multiple pairs of heavy socks wrapped in duffle, kept dry by moosehide moccasins, running to mid-calf, tied criss-crossed up my leg with moosehide thongs.

My hands were warm in beautiful moosehide mittens. The hide was thick enough to keep the cold and wind out. The mittens were lined with soft duffle to keep in the warmth. The wonderful thing about these mittens was the cuffs: they came up to the middle of my forearm. The elements could not get up my sleeves.

The cuffs were a marvel of beauty and winter technology. A three-petalled, beaded flower of green, red, yellow, and white adorned each of them. The detail was intricate, with the beads taking the shape of the petal in shrinking curves until converging into a tri-circle of green, gold, and red. The cuffs themselves were tapered. This allowed them to easily accommodate parka sleeves while closely holding the wrist. My parka sleeve formed a seal against the wind and cold.

As a boy, I would have called them "idiot mittens," because a multicoloured yarn rope connected the mittens in exactly the same way a piece of yarn had connected my boyhood mittens. The rope went behind my neck, outside my parka hood, allowing me to take my hands out of the mittens to let them dangle in place until needed again. The string on my boyhood mittens ran through my sleeves, eliminating the possibility of losing them. I hated that string then, but appreciated the useful variation now.

These mittens were such a blend of beauty and practicality that I had sent several pairs to friends as gifts. Most, too awed to make use of them, simply found a prominent place to display their unique, handmade beauty. They were certainly unique in a society where mittens were utilitarian and bought from piles in a bargain store. One couple asked me to send a second pair. I assumed these mittens were keeping my friends' hands warm. They had written an interesting question: "Is moosehide waterproof?"

This cold morning, I was on my way to have that question answered by the woman who had made the mittens. My visit would serve two purposes: I would find an answer for my friends and I would have a visit with a friend.

My walk took me on a road running along the Moose River appropriately named "River Road." The road was one of three on Moose Factory Island in the middle of the river. A town of some 2,000 souls was built there on Hudson's Bay Company history and Cree culture. The Crees were native people of the Algonquin group caught between a life of living off the land and the modern world of regular jobs and video games. Moosehide mittens were one of many subtle links holding these two worlds together.

I was walking to Sophia's home. She had made the mittens. I had no idea how old Sophia was at the time, but she was old. Her snow-white hair was always up in a bun. Her eyes were sunken, shining and jet-black, keenly observant and knowing. Her cheekbones and nose protruded with age hinting at the beauty of youth. Wrinkles, from almost a century of cold winter wind and hot summer sun, lined her face. On Moose Factory Island, these were signs of wisdom and experience.

I saw Sophia's house just off the road up ahead. A line of smoke rose into the morning sky from her chimney, connecting her home with dozens of her neighbours in that layer of haze, the by-product of early morning warmth. From a distance, her house looked like it was built of brick. As I got closer, I could see holes in the brick exposing huge, hand-hewn, squared logs that had been set a century before. The brick was actually asphalt shingle made to look like brick. Someone years before had decided that a brick façade would look better, perhaps more modern, than the ancient logs. Having no bricks, the next best thing was used—Insulbrick. The logs were natural, formed with muscle and sweat. The Insulbrick was manufactured and deteriorated in the weather. The squared logs held firm.

Sophia's roof was tin—long sheets to repel precipitation. Snow did not sit on the tin roof but was piled around the house, having slid off when the weight reached mini-avalanche proportions. I could see the snow piled around

Sophia's house. These snow piles were no accident. Each house had snow piled against the walls, despite the fact that many had a deeper layer of snow on the roof. Piled snow insulated a house from the rigours of cold and wind. Sophia's house was piled high with openings cut in the snowbank for her windows. Her snow was not piled as neatly as others' because a recent roof avalanche marred the handiwork of some boy she had paid to bank the snow against her home.

As I got closer to the house, I could see the sagging garage, which had at one time housed, in succession, dogsleds, snowmobiles, and pickup trucks. Now it was empty except for a few garbage bags waiting to be hauled to the dump.

I paused at the steps to the side porch. No one here used the front door. Sophia's was impassable, buried under the thick bank of protecting snow. If I had not seen the house in the summer, I would not have known there *was* a front door. The side porch was hanging a little askew from the house. Supported by corner posts on the ground, its list came from years of frost heaves. The side attached to the house was solid. The side on posts moved up and down subject to the whim of frost. Two weathered wooden steps led to the door. The door was in the backside of the porch so that winds off the river could not accompany a visitor into the house. Opening away from the house, the door was pulled crooked by its own weight on hinges loosened by swinging open too wide.

Pausing, I realized that I was losing my nerve. This question about the moosehide would seem ridiculous to Sophia. Maybe she would be upset that I had sent the mittens away.

Sophia had a keen sense of humour and the freedom to say whatever she wanted to say that only age can give. My hope was that she would explain how to care for moosehide. My fear was that she would not.

I opened the porch door, having made the first marks in the new fallen snow on the steps. The door swung to its odd hang, and I looked in. On a hook at the back of the porch hung some ptarmigan, undoubtedly a gift from a nephew to show his love and demonstrate his hunting ability. I could imagine Sophia cleaning them at her kitchen table. I could almost taste that woodstove-roasted fowl.

Icicles hung from the porch ceiling. Frost covered the walls. Each time the inside door opened, moisture escaped to freeze on porch walls and ceiling, forming a cavern-like appearance. I walked up the stairs and knocked on the door.

A light-green curtain hung in the door window. I could see a form on the other side, so I knew Sophia was there. While I was thinking of how to phrase my question, the curtain pulled back, and there was Sophia smiling at me. Her eyes were shining. She had a broad smile that revealed crooked teeth with two gold caps on the front right. She asked, "Is it you?"

"Yes, it's me," I replied.

"Well, come in." Sophia opened the door, stepping behind it as it swung. "You can't stand on the porch blabberskiting on a day like this. You'll freeze."

I stepped into Sophia's kitchen in a cloud of frost as frigid air hit moist kitchen warmth. The warmth enveloped me. The cloud dissolved. I felt at home.

Underpinnings as ancient as the log walls, but tired from battling frost and flood, were giving a tilt in several different directions to Sophia's kitchen floor. Faded and cracked linoleum covered that floor, emphasizing the undulations. A white porcelain sink with ancient, pockmarked fixtures ran the length of one wall, seemingly supported by a curtain that ran its length, and undoubtedly hiding cleaners and pots and pans.

A large, black wood stove with a warming bin above and a water reservoir to the side took up most of another wall. The heat in the kitchen radiated from that stove. A kettle rested on one side of the stove, away from the firebox, promising a warm cup of tea.

The other wall was taken up with a yellow wooden table and four matching chairs. Three were usable. The fourth was pinned against the wall behind the table. A red and white checked vinyl tablecloth covered the top. On the wall side of the table sat a vase with plastic roses, a small bowl of sugar, a pair of salt and pepper shakers, and a small picture of Jesus knocking on a door.

Sophia shuffled toward the parlour door. She was slightly bent with the weight of age. But mostly, she was suffering from arthritis and moving with sensible care. The parlour door framed a new scene. At the window I had passed on my walk, there was another wooden table strewn with sewing materials. Here there were two chairs, one on each side of the window. Only now did I realize how Sophia had come so quickly to the door. She had watched my arrival from her window seat and had shuffled to the kitchen door in preparation for my knock.

There were three other pieces of furniture in the parlour. An overstuffed, wide-armed easy chair sat on one side of the room covered with a handmade throw. A beautiful, mirrored sideboard filled another wall. Toward the centre of the room was an oil space heater radiating more warmth. It looked like a tall garbage can with an ornate top. A thin pipe left the top of the heater carrying fumes and smoke. A thinner pipe entered the heater at the bottom bringing oil to the firebox. The stovepipe went across the room at an upward angle and entered a box to safely carry the heat from the stove through the ceiling.

I pondered the wandering stovepipe, having seen it in many Cree homes. It dawned on me that the elongated stovepipe drained off as much heat as possible before expelling smoke into the cold air. Snare wire wrapped around the pipe and twisted to hooks screwed into the ceiling held the entire contraption in place.

Sophia motioned toward the second chair at the table as she settled into her chair by the window. I sat down. Immediately she began to bead. Her gnarled hands deftly plucked tiny beads off the table with a needle, sliding them onto a thread in one smooth motion. The needle flashed through a piece of moosehide, securing one more line to an intricate flower. The flower was identical to the one on my mittens and on those that I had sent as gifts.

The piece of material Sophia held was small. She embroidered the flowers on a portion of the cuff and then attached that to the mitten. Those aged fingers worked by rote at the task that must have been as familiar as breathing. Sophia didn't look up as she talked.

"Cold."

"Yes," I replied, wondering how to begin.

"Did you walk?"

"Well, yes; it's a nice morning." I would have thought it obvious that I had walked, since there was no vehicle outside.

"Van frozen?"

There was a bright red van, a donation, used for all kinds of work including visiting. Although there were only about two miles of roads on the island, I often found it most efficient to drive to meetings and homes. Was Sophia implying that I would not have walked unless the van was incapacitated?

"It's good to walk along the river. You can think."

Here was a potential segue to my question.

"I was thinking about these mittens while I was walking over here. They are beautiful and warm. They've been great all winter. I have a question about them."

Sophia got up and shuffled into the kitchen, returning with the teapot from the wood stove and a plate of cookies. She set both on the table.

"We need the cups," she said, pointing with her lips. This gesture had become familiar since my arrival on Moose Factory Island. A quick pucker of the lips and tilt back of the head was a means of pointing. I had no idea how this custom developed, but I had heard lots of warnings not to point a finger at certain islands or trees or cliffs because it was bad luck. Maybe pointing a finger anytime was impolite. So, people pointed lips.

I turned and saw two cups, one inside the other on a stack of two saucers, perched on the edge of the sideboard. There were cloth napkins as well. I stood to bring these items to the table.

Sitting down at my place once again, I watched Sophia separate the cups and saucers and begin to pour the tea. Her hand was steady.

"I was thinking about the mittens and the snow," I began again.

"We'll need the sugar." She pointed again.

I rose once more and turned to see a delicate, cut-glass creamer and sugar bowl on a matching plate sitting on the sideboard. I carefully picked up the set and placed it on the table, sitting down once again.

"I wanted to ask you a question about how to use the mitts." Nobody said mittens on the island. They were mitts. I suddenly realized that I was not sounding like the intelligent man I suspected Sophia thought I was.

"We'll need the spoons." Sophia's lips puckered and head tilted back. The two actions were simultaneous as far as I could tell. I stood and turned to see two delicate teaspoons on the sideboard. They were shiny and old with ornate handles. Sophia was, even for this simple visit, putting out her best for me. Suddenly, I felt honoured and nervous.

As I sat down, I looked more closely at the cups and saucers. They were delicate, bone china, cream-coloured with a pink pastel flower pattern. The saucers had scalloped edges. The cups had delicate handles with a slight flare at the top. These were antiques. They were beautiful and valuable. I wasn't sure if I should mention their beauty, so I said nothing.

Sophia passed my cup with a spoon on the saucer. She offered me the cream and sugar. She pointed to the plate of cookies. The cookie plate matched the cups.

I put a teaspoon of sugar in my cup and stirred.

"American."

I glanced up and saw her eyes twinkling; her smile revealed gold-capped teeth.

She was pouring cream into her tea.

I picked up the cup, holding it in both hands, "Cold American."

Sophia smiled and waited.

"Well, I worry about my mitts getting wet. Is moosehide waterproof?" I was not sure that waterproof was quite the term I wanted to use, but the question was out. I waited for Sophia to start laughing. I waited for a response like, "It keeps the moose dry." But Sophia recognized the question for exactly what it was.

She lowered her cup, which had been almost to her mouth, paused for a moment, and stood up. Expecting some kind of a remark, this surprised me. Sophia, leaning on the table a bit, shuffled around to where I was sitting, took my arm and applied enough pressure to indicate that I should stand up. I wondered if she was going to usher me to the door for asking a stupid question, but this seemed unlikely. Once standing, Sophia turned me around. I was still in my parka.

On Moose Factory Island, the custom was to leave outdoor attire on at all times when not at home, although opened for comfort. My assumption had always been that this was because many of the houses were old and drafty. The lean of Sophia's home in several directions at once created many cracks to the outside. It was certainly old and drafty. Besides that, the Cree did not have closets or, at least, not many in a house. Coats, when they were taken off, were hung on hooks on the back of the door. Usually, when visiting, there was nowhere to put a coat if you took if off. So, you left it on.

As I stood at Sophia's gentle insistence, my mittens dropped on either side of me on their string. The string was long enough to allow for a little slack when wearing them with my arms stretched out full length. Standing behind me, Sophia took each mitten, pulled them behind me and apparently wrapped them over each other, for they stayed behind me. I could feel the string taunt against my shoulders. I could feel the mittens gently pressing against my lower back. Then she apparently undid the mittens and let them hang. She took them once again and secured them behind my back.

"Now you," she said, undoing the mittens behind my back.

I placed the mittens behind my back and looped them over each other.

"Only once."

They stayed in place. I leaned forward. There were no mittens dangling in front of my face. The string had a more important role than either my mother or I had realized. I clumsily undid the mittens and let them fall to my side. I tried the whole procedure again. The trick to keeping the string around my neck with the mittens behind me was to make sure that it went under my arms and was fairly tight. Wrapping the mittens was backwards behind my back, so it was awkward, but I got the point.

"Thanks, Sophia." I was genuinely pleased, thinking of how all outdoor activities had just been revolutionized for me. "I never thought of that."

Her bright, black eyes grasped mine.

"If an Indian is going to get his hands wet, he takes his mitts off." Sophia shuffled to her chair, sat down, and took a sip of tea.

A History Lesson

He was old and stubborn when I met him. After two heart attacks and a stroke, he summarily ignored advice like, "Gilbert, it's time to slow down." Realistic about his health, Gilbert pressed on with life. His face had a thin, paunchy look accentuated by erratically placed teeth. Old, battered glasses formed a platform for long wisps of thinning white hair in varying degrees of genuflection to all points of the compass. Red patches of broken blood vessels on nose and cheeks decorated his aging, weathered skin, testifying to a relationship with whisky.

Gilbert was a hunter, a reader, and, above all else, a talker, making it his business to know a little about everything. He always claimed to have a doctorate in life, discussing any subject with an air of certainty, imparting enough information as to seem knowledgeable. Wily and wise, he cautiously avoided depth in conversations for fear of drowning.

Awards and interviews flowed to Gilbert because of his willingness to share on any subject. Poised on the edge of two cultures in an age of bridge building, Gilbert found himself in great demand with anyone remotely interested in Native Americans. Travelling the country as an expert on this or that, he learned more to support future travels, so he could vote here or advise there.

Gilbert was superficial, not insincere. He would speak from his heart, somehow relating every subject to his Cree heritage. He offered listeners a glimpse of Cree life and culture previously seen only by academics of the anthropological persuasion. The world outside his life and village was his foil, a background upon which to paint a picture of his beloved Crees.

Instinctively, Gilbert knew that listeners would interact best with what related to their norm, their standards, their experience. And so, he learned from the world exactly what he needed to help the world learn from him.

Gilbert was willing to speak anywhere: political rallies, church gatherings, educational forums, and interest clubs alike. Whether or not his endless supply of anecdotal material, exactly appropriate for every nuance of every subject, was fact or fiction never seemed an issue. Every example, every situation generously seasoning Gilbert's talks had the ring of experience. Each story, each glimpse of Cree life, shed a beam of light on a point of intersection, a point of potential understanding, between two cultures. People left Gilbert's presentations pleased to know a bit more about his culture and astonished at new insights into their own.

Gilbert received not only invitations to events all over the country, but phone calls and visits from organizations from around the world. Some wanted advice for a project. Others hoped to find precedents for a cause. Still others simply wanted to learn more about some aspect of Cree life and history. Gilbert obliged them all.

Cree history is intertwined with the fur trade. Fur built the retail supply lines from England and Europe through northern Canada, fostering early missionary efforts in North America. Much study surrounded trade and church as they affected Cree life in the inhospitable north. Gilbert was a living encyclopedia on the subject.

Moose Factory Island, at the southern tip of James Bay in northern Ontario, was the perfect place for research. Accessible by train for modern-day explorers, it was an early centre for European trade and church in North America. Historically, goods were off-loaded at the Hudson Bay docks and shipped all over north America. Dog team in winter and schooner in summer carried the necessities of life over the James and Hudson bays.

For the eighteenth-century explorer, faraway places meant wealth and new lands to colonize. For the twentieth-century explorer, any town inaccessible by road was exotic and interesting. Gilbert understood this, becoming a teller of tales, skillfully weaving threads of the past onto the warp of modern life, creating a colourful fabric in great demand.

One group of historical anthropologists came to Moose Factory Island intent on picking up the trail of Henry Hudson and his men along the shores of the bay bearing his name. Early Hudson's Bay Company reports of fair-haired, fair-skinned native children drew this small group of scholars from the safety of the University of Toronto. Armed with bits of an ambiguous puzzle about the castaways, this naive research team hoped Gilbert would fit the pieces together. Two men and a woman, all scholars, all thrilled to be in the field, stopped by Gilbert's home on the edge of the Moose Factory Reserve to interview the native historian.

Moose Factory Island had three distinct residential sections. The southern end was for "southerners." Staff for the regional hospital, government workers, and school personnel, all from parts elsewhere, were provided housing on this part of the island. In the centre of the island, the non-status native people had built homes. These were primarily descendants of Hudson's Bay staff or natives from other villages who had relocated to Moose Factory. A small Hudson's Bay enclave had occupied a place on this part of the island for more than 100 years. As well, the Anglican church and residence were built here, testament to the link between commerce and prayer. The third section of the island was reserved for members of the Moose Factory Band. Although no physical demarcations existed, the three divisions were obvious to every resident.

For the most part, the division of Moose Factory Island was a pragmatic solution to a housing problem. Sources of residential funding defined the sectional boundaries. In the southern section, housing was provided by the government or school district. On the reserve, the Band administered housing funds from government grants. Those living in the centre of the island fended for themselves.

The government houses were like those found on military bases anywhere in the world. Homes provided by the school were of the single-family variety, resembling double-wide mobile units. Native houses were plywood and frame boxes, forming a miniature suburban sprawl. These two sections had straight, planned, orderly roads running north to south and east to west.

The centre section was different. Each home was built to taste and budget. There were two-storey homes built to use heat efficiently. There were sprawling ranch-style homes and tiny box houses. There were even elaborate tent frames reserving land until a permanent dwelling could be afforded. When this section of the island was being established, there was no need for orderly roads. People lived where there was room, usually near family. In the sixties, it became necessary to make order from the squatters' chaos to provide services such as fire protection and garbage pickup. Streets were built through the maze of homes. Where homes blocked the forward progress of a street, a cul-de-sac was built. People were easier to find in the two end sections of Moose Factory, but the centre section seemed more vibrant.

Gilbert, an exceptional person, had built an exceptional house on the edge of the reserve. His was the first house on the reserve, making him easy to find. There was Willie's house, the last of the non-native houses, then the baseball field, and then Gilbert's home and the reserve. Gilbert's house was exceptional in that he built it to taste and necessity, rejecting plans used by virtually everyone else on the reserve.

The small band of researchers, having completed their journey from Toronto first by car, then 200 miles by train, and finally crossing the Moose River in a freighter canoe, made their way from the dock down the dusty Center Road to Gilbert's home. They were expected. This might not have been a good thing. Gilbert had had time to prepare. Assuming that I was a scholar in my own right, Gilbert invited me to his home to meet the research team. I think he felt more comfortable, despite his diplomatic aplomb, with another southern, white person present for the initial meeting. In time, I also came to understand that Gilbert wanted a witness.

I arrived early for the interview. Gilbert was subdued but enthusiastic.

"This will be interesting," he informed me. "These are experts on the history of the area. They just want some detail about Hudson once he hit land near Rupert's house."

"Do you know about Henry Hudson and his men?" I asked, caught up in spite of myself, momentarily forgetting to whom I was speaking.

"Some. There's not a lot to know."

When the knock came, Gilbert opened the door, welcoming everyone. I noticed that the open door didn't add much light to the already bright room. Huge corner windows with multiple panes of glass made the room warm and cheery. Gilbert's house was small. This room was a dining room, living room and meeting place. The five of us must have approached the legal occupancy limit.

"Come on in and sit down. Can I get you some tea?"

Gilbert was beaming, sincerely pleased to welcome his visitors. His offer of tea betrayed his nervousness. Gilbert was a staunch follower of native social tradition. Native social tradition dictated that tea was served at the end of a visit.

Before anyone could find a seat at the table, Gilbert introduced me.

"This is our rector. He has a keen interest in the history of the area."

We shook hands, with each person identifying himself or herself.

"Hi, I am Karen Trotter, teaching fellow at the U of T."

"Russell Simpson, nice to meet you."

"Bill Mizable—glad to sit down."

This was a nice group of people. Karen seemed the youngest, possibly in her mid-thirties. Russell and Bill were typical academics, wire-rimmed glasses and all, both in their forties. Each came armed with a notepad just in case the other did not record things quite accurately. Karen had a small tape recorder. Russell had a camera.

"We appreciate you taking the time to see us, Gilbert," Bill began as the other two interviewers surreptitiously surveyed the room and house beyond.

Gilbert was a small-talk expert.

"Always happy to learn a little more about this area. And I intend to pick your brains. Did you know the bridge at Moose River is the only example in Canada of an inverted suspension structure?" Gilbert asked as he informed. "So you all are with the anthropology department at the University of Toronto?"

"Actually," Karen replied, "we are all from different departments. I am history. Bill is anthropology. And we aren't sure what Russ does."

Russ laughed. "I'm in the bursar's office. Just came along for the ride. Bill and I have travelled together a bit. He writes. I take pictures. How long have you been living here, Father?"

"Its Canon," Gilbert interjected. "He's a son of a gun." The honorary title, given by the church for faithful service, was a never-ending source of jokes such as: "He's pretty high calibre," or "Maybe that's why we see him loaded so often." Gilbert couldn't resist.

Embarrassed, I laughed. "I was here for a year about seven years ago and couldn't stay away. I've been here three years this second time."

"Are you the pastor of the church that floats away?" Bill asked.

"Well—" I began.

"Yes, but that's another story." Gilbert completed my sentence, preserving his right to another information session. "Canon Collins is our Anglican minister."

"History buff?" Karen asked.

I looked at Karen and thought briefly. "Just interested in everything."

Nellie, Gilbert's wife, whom I hadn't seen yet, appeared with a tray holding cups, a kettle, and a plate of cookies. Her grey hair was done in a tight perm accentuating the roundness of her smiling face. Her eyes, bright and friendly, lighted on each face in the group, stopping for an extra moment at Gilbert. She filled the room with a palpable sense of joy.

"Tea and cookies. We won't talk here today without tea and cookies. How are you, Jim? Did you walk all the way up here to listen to Gilbert tell another tale?"

"No," I replied. "I came for the tea and cookies."

"Another tale?" Gilbert feigned anger and hurt. "Leave the tray and be gone, woman."

Everyone laughed at the exchange. If the visitors caught the not-so-subtle warning in Nellie's quip, they didn't let on. Nellie poured just the right amount of milk and then the tea. With tea to fill awkward pauses and occupy hands, everyone relaxed. The conversation drifted from the Polar Bear Express, rail link to the south, to the beauty of the countryside.

Gilbert, as self-declared resident expert, rolled the dice of discussion. "Your interest in Henry Hudson, where has it led you before tea in my kitchen?"

"Well," Karen began. "We all caught the bug after seeing some artifacts displayed by the Cree Regional Authority during Native Education Week."

Now this was interesting. "What artifacts?" I asked.

Russ looked at his companions for approval as he recited a list of display items. "There was a sextant, a beautiful hand compass, a brass water bottle and a flintlock pistol. Right?"

"Yes!" Bill chimed in, as if on cue. "We were told they were all from the Rupert's House area, brought by a group of men in a small boat. A least, that's the oral tradition."

"We assume the boat was used with local logs to build a winter shelter for the group. Does that make sense?" Karen attempted to draw an answer from Gilbert.

Gilbert moved through conversations on his own terms. "Do you folks know anything about native visiting traditions?"

The group responded with a variety of negative nods, obviously concerned about breaching some time-honoured visitation rite.

"Well, we usually serve tea just before everyone leaves. But we know that Wemistigoshoo likes tea and talk, so Nellie brought it, and we had better drink it before she takes it away."

Nellie pretended to be horrified in a way that looked real to me. "Gilbert!" She gasped and scolded, "Don't be so rude. Were you raised in the bush?"

"Yes, as a matter of fact I was. And so were you."

I was enjoying the banter, but the little learning expedition was uncomfortable. "Well, Nellie, no matter where you were raised, you make the best oatmeal cookies in Canada. I was raised in Pittsburgh and we had to wait for the hostess to begin." I passed the plate of cookies to Nellie.

"Jim is supposed to be polite. He's a minister. I'm supposed to be blunt and grouchy, because I'm Indian and an elder."

I couldn't help but laugh at Gilbert and his gap-toothed smile.

"Well, you do a good job, Keshailo," Nellie affirmed, lifting her teacup. Meaningless to the visitors, the endearment "Old Man" carried for Gilbert and Nellie a half-century of devotion.

Gilbert launched into the conversation. "Smart men would have used the boat for shelter of some kind. A small boat would do them no good anyway. Where could they go? The Indians had canoes more suited to the conditions on the Bay. Why not use it."

"So finding the remains of a shelter would be possible?" Karen asked with expectation.

My interest was piqued once again. Everyone looked at Gilbert. Would this be a simple matter of unearthing a crude cabin?

"No."

Gilbert might as well have given a lengthy diatribe on the vast cost of an archeological dig on the James Bay. Everyone relaxed, deflated. If conversation for Gilbert was like fishing, he had just selected his bait.

"Nothing on an island near the bank escapes the river for more than a decade. And chances are if these men landed, they stopped on the first island they hit and made a shelter on the first piece of bank they could climb. They didn't know the Bay." This sounded ominous, but intriguing.

Gilbert drew me in. "What do you mean, Gilbert?" I asked.

"As you travel around here on the river, you can see how the banks are cut every spring by the ice. The river tears down here and builds up somewhere else. Even the old Cretien Frere fort that was here is gone. Hell, Charles Island loses twenty or thirty feet every year. You've seen breakup, Jim."

"It's amazing. The power and size of the ice chunks pushed by spring thaw flooding the river," I explained in earnest awe of breakup.

Nellie, with characteristic mirth, chimed in. "Breakup is like a party, here. Everyone watches the river. We have breakup contests and picnics on the bank to watch the ice. Everything stops when the river begins to break. We even leave church if breakup starts during a service."

Nellie unwittingly became Gilbert's cheerleader. Her enthusiasm renewed interest in Henry Hudson's fate, despite the knowledge there would be no log dwelling found, and even though she was enthusiastic about a totally unrelated subject.

Ignoring the information about breakup festivities, Karen jumped right back into the reason for her travel to Moose Factory.

"So you know about Henry Hudson's landing on the coast? You have heard the stories?"

Under less exciting circumstances, Karen might have thought before she spoke. Her questions, in the form of statements, delivered with unbridled enthusiasm became exclamations. Crees asking information, in the interest of being polite, often phrase questions in such a way as to assume a negative response. That way the answer, if negative, always sounds positive. To the question, "I can't borrow your rifle, can I?" "Yes" is a negative response. The full response would be "Yes, you can't borrow my rifle." Conversely, the full positive response would be "No, you can borrow my rifle." Properly asked, Karen's question would have been framed, "You don't know about Henry Hudson's landing on the coast, do you?"

Gilbert could have responded, "Yes, I don't," or "No, I do."

As it was, Gilbert was on the spot. If he didn't know anything, he would have to answer "no" instead of "yes." But Gilbert would not be put on the spot.

"What are you interested in knowing?" He answered a question with a question.

And again he did it. "How could something that happened over two hundred years ago be so important?"

Russell answered this time, his sincere enthusiasm infectious.

"Its just fascinating. People making a journey of that magnitude in what we would consider a large cabin cruiser, and then surviving, being set adrift to become the great, great-grandparents of red- and blond-haired native children. It's really the collision of two cultures under completely improbable circumstances that is interesting. We don't care about proving anything, we just want to learn."

Bill, who had been quietly drinking his tea and eating the tiny sugar cookies offered by Nellie, commented in passing.

"The influence of English and European traders is well documented. There are probably lots of descendants of early company men here on the island. But there really is nothing about Henry Hudson and his crew. The thought that they might now be part of the gene pool from a coastal community is intriguing."

"Any nail in the can will hold the board," Gilbert offered from nowhere.

This off-handed bit of local wisdom halted the conversation. Was Gilbert dismissing the importance of Henry Hudson's men having descendants, or was he speaking of genetic assimilation? Personally, I thought Gilbert had been saving that line for years and had finally found a circumstance that fit.

"Well," Gilbert began in a quiet voice, "I can tell you what was I told by my granny."

Gilbert had cast his line. The visitors were speechless with hope and gratitude.

"There are a lot of tales told in the goose camp, but you can't call them history."

Gilbert was trolling for an academic northern pike.

"Comparing local stories is often how a picture of the past is painted." Karen was coming up behind the bait.

Russell was not far behind. "Local stories often inform the historical record."

Bill took the bait for the whole team. "We could enjoy more tea and cookies while you tell us what your granny told you. It would be a privilege to hear one of your family stories."

Nellie's eyes were twinkling. She knew Gilbert had a strike.

"I would love to hear this, too. Let me freshen the pot. Don't start, Keshailo," Nellie instructed, "until I get back."

I doubted anyone missed the loving tease of sarcasm in her voice.

"Well, all I can do is tell you what I was told as a boy. You know, before the kids had television, the elders were our entertainment. I spent lots of hours listening to my granny. That's how I learned. My granny was old when I was a boy, so this might be a first-hand account."

"If that's the case," Karen quipped, demonstrating an unwillingness to be reeled in too far from the truth, "she was very old when she told you the story."

"Well there wasn't much pollution then, and Granny ate a lot of bear grease," Gilbert came right back, letting us know he was not prepared to catch and release.

"Granny said that a small boat, pointed at both ends, landed on the beach near what used to be the Old Factory post. That is just south of Eastmain on a modern map."

There was a general scuffle at the table while Russell unfolded a map of northern Quebec. I could see that this was a topographical map. That made sense, because Eastmain was hundreds of miles from the nearest road. The fleur-de-lys in the corner indicated that it had been published by the Quebec government. I was impressed. This group came prepared.

Gilbert peered at the map spread on the table over plates and cups.

"Here. Old Factory was in that bay there. See, here is Eastmain. So the boat landed somewhere between here and here."

His wrinkled, scarred finger traced a shaky path down a short piece of Quebec shoreline.

"Apparently the boat was swamped. Probably by breakers as they pulled in to the beach. Every hunter knows that the breakers, in shallow, will swamp a boat over the stern if you don't run to the beach properly."

Each member of the group was writing on his and her pad. "Boat swamped over the stern running to beach," I supposed was written in three different versions. This seemed a good illustration for a sermon on differing gospel accounts of the same event.

Gilbert went on, encouraged by the note taking.

"That water is cold. Even though this supposedly happened in midsummer. My granny called it 'Wapmeckopisma' or 'white whale month,' because that's when lots of beluga whales came. We don't use that name, but I think it was August."

Pens and pencils raced.

"These men, I don't remember how many, were nearly starved and dying of thirst. A couple of hunters saw the boat and ran to the village with the news. Remember, they had never seen a boat like that. For that matter, they had never seen white men. Anyway, a whole group of villagers came back. They were scared, but willing to help. I guess they knew what it was like to be swamped."

He forged ahead with vocal variations that would be the envy of any radio announcer.

In a low voice, Gilbert described his granny's description of the limp, almost lifeless men being lifted from the boat. With admiration, he explained the process of building a huge, warming fire on the beach. He expressed the wonder and awe of isolated villagers unloading the boat and finding things never before seen. Surprisingly enough, those things included the very items mentioned by the inquisitive college personnel sitting across from Gilbert hanging on every historic word.

What luck for the researchers that Gilbert's granny had mentioned the things that had stimulated their search. This could be physical proof of a legend. A momentary flash of cynicism caused me to flick an involuntary glance at Nellie. She had a slight smile. Her eyes gave away her thoughts, dancing from Gilbert to each member of the team. I wondered whether Gilbert was embellishing his story for realism's sake or reeling in a stringer full.

He went on to describe the concern of the men upon discovering that their belongings, including weapons, were missing. Great emphasis was placed upon the various facial expressions and physical gesticulations employed in bridging the linguistic gap between European and native. This confirmed my suspicions. I had never heard any fairytale include detailed descriptions of body language.

Gilbert described what could only be called a "skit" performed by Henry Hudson and his men to depict the eviction from his ship. Apparently, Henry Hudson had unwittingly invented the game of charades.

"And so some of the men had their hands behind their back and some pushed them into the boat." Gilbert finished his description of the impromptu one-act play.

"Everyone seemed to understand. My granny said that the chief made the men understand that they should follow him. They did. Some of the people carried everything from the boat to the village. Remember this was the first time they had seen white men, that type of boat, the clothes, anything. I don't think the Canadian government would be as friendly to aliens, do you?"

Before anyone could answer, Gilbert went on. "The village was not too far from the shore. My great, great-grandfather didn't have to hide from enemies. The village was just high enough to avoid even the highest breakup flood."

I was beginning to relax, but I could see that Nellie was still laughing inside. Gilbert was adding a little too much detail for this to be a "told around the fire tale."

"There was a big celebration in the little village. Everyone had come out to see the strangers. It was an exciting thing to have visitors in the village, but especially visitors so obviously different. Children were frightened by the appearance of the Europeans. Young women were immediately enamoured of the their exotic look. Then the villagers did a very Cree thing."

Gilbert sipped his tepid tea.

"What did they do?" Karen asked breathlessly, as if she were at the top of the first drop of a roller coaster.

"They put them in a pot and ate them."

Everyone sat in stunned silence except for Nellie.

Giggling, she offered little comfort, "I warned you."

I decided to try to lighten the moment for the intrepid visitors. "Well, at least we know they didn't come to push their religion on the Crees."

Everyone looked at me. "Well, come on! It's obvious. If they were thrown in a pot, they couldn't have been friars."

Russ began to laugh, while his teammates still sat shocked.

"It might have been easier for you to say that our search was silly, but this has been a lot of fun," said Russ with an embarrassed laugh.

Gilbert's response was direct: "Some things we need to know to know more, and some things we don't need to know to know more."

The Signal

The Moose River empties into the southern tip of the James Bay in northern Ontario. In the centre of the river sits Moose Factory Island, named for both the river and the manager of the Hudson's Bay Company. His official title is "Factor." His house is the "factory."

In the summer, the short trip to the island from the Ontario Northland railhead, in the town of Moosonee, is made by canoe—not the small craft that is paddled, but a large, square-stern boat driven by a powerful, outboard motor. The length of the canoe ride varies with the tide. At low tide, the taxi must head downstream, skirting an exposed sandbar in the middle of the river. At high tide, the canoe travels straight across the river, over the sandbar, and through a man-made gap in Charles Island to weave around the back end of Sawpit Island, ending the trip at the hospital docks.

In the winter, with three feet of ice built up across the river, trucks and cars can drive straight from the Misawenikan Hall hill on the Moosonee side, across Charles Island, through the provincial park, and up the boat ramp near Ray's house on Moose Factory Island.

Both of these routes are impassable in the spring and the fall. In years gone by, brave souls crossed ice melting in the spring thaw by walking beside a boat they slid over the ice. If the ice gave way, they jumped into the boat. In the fall, then and now, people who appear to lack good sense, but who know the river, cross over what seems to be a skim of ice, walking gingerly at low tide across sections of the river with little current. Helicopters now ferry less adventurous citizens of the island back and forth to the mainland when the river is impassable.

Alex had lived on the island all his life, working for the Hudson's Bay Company. As a young boy, he had served, in the summer, on the sailing sloops that carried goods from Moose Factory to communities along the James and Hudson bays. In the winter, he had attended school on the island.

The school, Horden Hall, was named after the first bishop of the area. Alex and other children from the island attended during the day. Children from across the James Bay lived at the school, having been taken from their villages to be educated in a standard acceptable in the South. Although the officials who devised the residential school system for the native children of isolated parts of Canada sincerely believed it was done as a means of efficiently educating the North, the damage done to the familial, cultural, and social structure of the native villages was permanent.

In his retirement, Alex was content to take the occasional handyman job on the island, working with the energy of a man half his age. When not employed, Alex worked around his house, cut wood and helped anyone he could in the village. If the Anglican church had any kind of a project, from painting to electrical repair, Alex volunteered.

For over a month in the early spring, a group of tireless workers dug, by hand, a basement under the church parish hall. Alex was not able to dig, but accepted the role of project supervisor without being asked. But the crew of volunteers went about their work according to their own plans, regardless of his directions, causing much blustering and the use of language certainly not related to the construction of a church hall. Invariably, the day after his ideas had been ignored, Alex would return to the project pleased with progress and armed with a new set of irrelevant directions.

On an isolated island with a small population, everyone knows everyone else. Alex was no exception. Everyone knew him. At a distance, he was recognizable in his green hunting cap, red plaid flannel jacket, and blue bib overalls. His hat was always askew, allowing a few wisps of white hair to escape and blow in the wind. Alex was bent with age, but still powerful. Large arms, built from years of heavy labour, were sagging but able to do more than their share of carrying blocks or wheelbarrowing cement. His bull neck, wrinkled with age, tensed against loads far heavier than one man should lift.

Despite being irritated by workers who ignored him, Alex displayed his sense of humour regularly. A quick smile was followed by a staccato laugh usually preceding a practical joke or a comment designed to emphasize someone's inadvertent mistake. I was the victim of his humour more than once.

As I paused to get more nails while framing a wall for the new basement, Alex asked me for my hammer. Puzzled, I looked at the hammer hanging from his work belt, but I gave him mine. I had a habit, when tired from hammering, of holding my hammer up from the end of the handle. This was the type of idiosyncrasy Alex loved. Without hesitation, he picked up a power saw and cut four inches off the wooden handle of my hammer.

"That was just added weight, since he didn't use that part anyway, him," he announced to the rest of the men, who were doubling over with laughter.

Handing me the hammer he observed, "You should be able to work faster now because this is more to your liking."

All I could do was laugh as I looked for another hammer.

One of the workmen dared to tell Alex that more spacers were needed for a section of framing that was being built.

In response to this innocuous request, Alex responded, "Alex has two speeds—slow and stop. Which one do you want?"

Despite the irascible temper and unexpected practical jokes, everyone enjoyed having Alex on the job. Ignored supervision notwithstanding, he was a hard worker, contributing a great deal to what was accomplished each day. So it was with mixed feelings that the crew received Alex's news that he was going to his cabin across the river while the ice was still good.

Many people on the island had built cabins on what was called "the Quebec side" of the Moose River. Built as bases for hunting and places to rest when cutting wood, they served primarily as a getaway destination when the bustle of life on the island became intolerable. Alex wanted to get to his cabin while the ice was still strong enough to hold a snow machine without any danger.

I had been to Alex's cabin that winter on a woodcutting expedition. It was a small, rectangular structure built out of two-by-sixes, logs and plywood. There was just one long room—one end for sleeping, and the other end for sitting. The middle was for cooking and eating. Glass windows, broken at some time in the past, had been replaced with plastic that let in the light but blocked the view. A short, squat, cast-iron wood stove radiated heat while offering a cooking surface big enough to hold every pot and pan on the island. One double bed, a table and two chairs, an overstuffed couch, and an almost matching overstuffed chair, both of which looked like two wildcats had been fighting on them, completed the décor of the cabin. On the door was a calendar from the 1960s with pictures of airplanes from that era. Oil lamps and candles placed strategically around the cabin provided light.

Someone visiting Alex might wonder why he would want to spend time at such a place—a ramshackle cabin, in the middle of a spruce forest, half a river away from the closest person.

Those were the reasons Alex wanted to get to his cabin while he could still travel. He had built the cabin decades before as a newlywed, thinking of romantic weekends away from the village. His children had contributed to the state of the windows and furniture over the years when they won the daily clamour to go to the "camp." Some of his grandchildren had spent time with him when they were younger, learning to light a wood stove and snare rabbits, but the lure of television and video games had long since rendered Alex's beloved camp boring. He didn't mind. Every visit to camp was etched in his memory. When he was there, they were there, too.

In the midst of the parish hall project, Alex hitched his sled to his snow machine, bought extra gas, loaded what he needed to stay at his cabin for a few weeks, and left. In southern society, an octogenarian attempting to camp in total isolation, in the wilderness, in temperatures well below freezing, would have been unthinkable. Alex's family noted that he was leaving, but they believed he had the right to do so, not to mention the skills to live in the bush by himself.

Alex was pulling a sled that had dozens of relatives on the island. Built primarily of plywood, one-half inch for the box and three-quarters of an inch for the floor, it rode on two ten-foot two-by-eights curved at the front end to form runners. In the old days, Alex would have smeared horse manure on the runners; frozen, it formed a slick surface to run over snow and ice. This particular sled had two-inch strips of tin tacked the full length of each runner for the same purpose. There were no longer horses on the island.

Everything Alex needed for a long stay at his camp was packed into the sled. The ice that Alex would be crossing was over three feet thick. The ice would break up when the pressure of melting snow from upstream forced it to break into huge chunks. Eventually, the flow would force the broken ice into the James Bay, allowing boat travel. Then, someone would bring Alex home. He would simply leave his snow machine at the camp until the river froze again.

With no way to know when the river would break up, the date and hour became the subject of a village pool and many individual bets. Once the river broke, there was no way to know how long it would take for the ice to flow out into the James Bay, opening the river for boat travel. Knowing this, Alex had taken supplies and equipment for a two-month stay at camp.

He had food, plenty of gas for his snow machine, a chain saw, and plenty of ammunition for both his rifle and his shotgun.

He left the village at first light to be certain that the he was across the river before the rising sun had time to thaw the ice, creating slush that could bog down his heavy sled. No one noticed his leaving. His sons knew that he was going, but as he made his way through the village to the river, the few people who heard the roar of his snow machine simply noted that someone was travelling.

Although my office was in my home, I walked each day the half-mile along River Road to St. Thomas Church. The 150-year-old building was within sight of the river. The church, built by Hudson Bay shipbuilders, had an interior shaped like the upside-down hull of a boat. Knowing the extent of flooding along the Moose River, normally flowing placidly in the distance, they had drilled holes in the church floor to air out the wooden underpinnings saturated by the floodwaters. Modern-day tourists were told that these holes were made to scuttle the church so that it would not float off its foundation when the waters rose.

In winter, the walk to the church was frigid, as the north wind blew freely down the length of the river from the James Bay. In the summer, the walk was restful, particularly in the evening with a blazing sunset reflected off the water. In the fall, the foliage along the river banks became a feast for the eyes, as the bright yellows of poplar and aspen blended into the reds of chokecherries and mooseberries laced with the green of spruce and tamarack. In the spring, the walk was downright exciting.

The days were lengthening. Although the ice was still thick on the river, the snow was gone from the ground. A circus-like atmosphere existed all across the island. Families were walking together. Children were playing in every open piece of land available. Everyone was anticipating breakup. As people walked along the river, they paused to see if there was any change in the ice. All night long, men patrolled the riverbanks, watching for the water to rise. If the spring thaw brought too much water, parts of the village could flood. The shoreline patrols could give people enough time to get to high ground or into the canoes stored behind their houses.

Because the river broke as water built up upstream, the southern end of the Moose River broke long before the river at the island. Twenty miles south of the island was the tiny town of Moose River Crossing. Half a century before, it had been a bustling lumber camp. Now there were a few homes and a store next to a bridge that crossed the river. Moose River Crossing was the only telephone contact along the river south of the island for almost two hundred miles. At breakup that phone contact was vital. Someone at the store would call to the island to announce that the river had broken. Within three days, breakup would progress to the island.

The force of the flood would push huge blocks of ice across low lands, sweeping trees, earth, and houses with it. Entire islands were cut away to be rebuilt farther upstream as the flood subsided. Alex knew this, and had built his cabin on ground high enough to avoid even the highest flood.

Alex was Metis—mixed blood. His heritage was Cree and European. The Crees had lived in northern Ontario since before memory. Europeans had come to the area a century and a half before to convert and trade. Half of the population of the island had this ancestry. Regardless of heritage, the land and the river were unforgiving of those who did not understand how to exist in the wilderness. For Alex and others who did understand, the land provided what was needed to live.

Breakup was spectacular the year that Alex left the basement project to stay at his camp. It happened in mid-afternoon, so the entire village turned out to watch in awe. As the flood rose, the pressure built up behind the ice until it exploded, throwing house-sized chunks into the air. Breakup moved foot by foot toward the mouth of the river to the thunder of exploding ice and the cheers of village onlookers.

It soon became apparent that there was too much water pushing the broken ice. The river was rising fast. Residents knew exactly what was happening. The push of water from upriver had forced the broken ice into a natural dam at the river's mouth, holding back the exaggerated flow. Town officials called an armed forces base 400 miles to the south, asking for assistance. Before the night was out, the ice dam had been bombed, allowing the river to flow into the James Bay. The waters subsided, making unnecessary dozens of canoes tied to porches all over the island.

The entire drama had taken only four days from the first call placed at Moose River Crossing until the river's flow had been released. There was no power on the island for another week, because ice had toppled a transmission tower two miles upriver. For that week, the island was thrown back in time. Those who depended on wood for heat opened their homes to those who did not, as warm spring days faded with the setting sun to frigid spring nights. Streetlights were dark. The soft glow of candles or the undulating light of oil lamps filled every home.

Alex knew that the breakup was unusual. He watched the flood wash away trees well away from the normal spring flow. Knowing the island was prepared for the emergency, he cut wood, hunted partridge, snared rabbits, and enjoyed the solitude of his camp. Alex had allowed himself one modern convenience: a portable radio, because his beloved Maple Leafs were in the Stanley Cup playoffs. Each night they played, he sat back in his threadbare easy chair, intent on the commentary.

While walking to the church the second Sunday after breakup, as I was watching chunks of ice drift by, I thought I saw smoke rising across the river.

The river was over half a mile wide on the east side of the island. I stopped and strained to see. There was no smoke. After the service, as I was walking home, I looked again at the spot on the opposite bank where I thought I had seen smoke. A line of smoke was clearly visible against the green of the trees behind. I watched for a few moments before walking on. By the time I arrived home, a glance across the river revealed a large plume of white/grey smoke easily visible across the distance. It looked like a small forest fire.

Isolated forest fires were fought only if there was potential danger to towns or individual dwellings. Fires that presented no danger were allowed to burn out. More than once, when flying over the bush in Northern Ontario during the summer, I had seen the smoke of a distant fire. In country full of marshes, lakes, and rivers, few of the isolated fires grew to any size. Once a fire had passed through an area, blueberries, raspberries, and other small ground plants thrived, providing forage for moose and treats for any passing bear. Nature, full of paradox, produced the destructive force of a forest fire that could stimulate new life.

Knowing that there was no chance of the fire's spreading across the river, I watched the smoke out of curiosity. At regular intervals, the grey smoke billowed thicker and higher only to die down for a while, and billow again. I could see that the fire was not growing, but burning in one place. There were no flames visible across the river, just masses of smoke. Just as I was about to go into the house, a helicopter passed overhead, flying toward the fire.

The helicopter hovered for a moment after reaching the opposite bank, and then landed near the fire. I could not tell if it landed on the ice or on the bank. As I watched, it took off again, flying back to the island. I went inside and called the police to find out what was happening. The fire had been a signal. The smoke had been seen by others who called the authorities. A signal meant an emergency, so a helicopter was dispatched from Moosonee. Someone had been brought into the hospital, but the police did not have a name.

Small towns have wireless, non-electronic communication systems that rival any high-tech equipment. Without asking, without even leaving the house or using the telephone, I was told that Alex had built the fire and had been brought back to the island. A young man who was delivering something for his mother, in preparation for a meeting later that evening, had all the news except what was wrong with Alex.

Out of concern, I called the hospital but was told that Alex had been discharged after a brief examination. He was fine. The hospital worker did not know why Alex had been brought back to the village. My curiosity about the fire had been satisfied. Surprised to find out about Alex, I was happy to know that he was all right. I decided to drop by his house the next day to find out why he needed to get back to the village.

Alex lived in a section of the island where non-status native people and status people from other towns lived. These people could not get land on the reserve, because they were not part of the Moose Factory Band. Traditionally, they had lived around the Hudson's Bay Post and the church. A mass of tents and cabins placed randomly in the centre section of the island had slowly turned to a confusing maze of small, single-storey homes of a more permanent nature. By the time I arrived on the island, dirt roads had been built in an attempt to bring order and infrastructure to the homes. The roads had no names but were identified by the name of the most prominent citizen living there. Because prominence is a relative thing, many roads were identified differently by different people. It was important to know everyone on every road or directions became quite abstruse.

Alex lived on a road that I called Faries Road. His house was small and square, with faded red shiplap siding. His yard was surrounded by a small picket fence that had, at one time, been white. The gate was gone. There was a second opening in the fence to accommodate a short gravel driveway that pointed from the road to a tiny garage matching the house.

Alex was in his yard stacking firewood. It was a beautiful day for a visit outside.

"Wachiya," he said, looking up and smiling.

"Wachiya," I responded. "It's a beautiful day. I thought I could take a nice walk and drop by for a visit at the same time. How is the camp?"

"Milawshin—it was good." Alex continued to stack wood. "But I am back now. I came back yesterday."

"I heard that you built the smoke and came back by helicopter yesterday." I was curious about what had happened but afraid Alex wouldn't want to talk about his trip home. He alleviated my concern.

"You saw it?"

"I think everyone saw it." I laughed. "Are you okay, Alex? Are you sick?"

"I'm fine, me," he said with a Moose Factory twang.

"Why did you need a helicopter? What was the fire for if you were okay?" I thought this might be too direct. Folks on the island spent a great deal of time talking around important subjects, working up to the point of the conversation.

"That fire was hard to light; the kindling and wood went up good, but the boughs were wet and wouldn't catch." Alex was talking about the fire, but skirting the subject. "I had to let the boughs dry over the fire for almost an hour before I got any smoke."

I realized that this must have been what I saw on the way to church. "Yeah, I thought I saw campfire smoke when I was walking to church."

"There's not enough smoke," Alex explained, "without green boughs, but, until they catch, they only break up the smoke so you can't see it. We used to do that working in the bush as boys." Still avoiding my question, he offered an interesting piece of history. "At school in Chapleau, we cut firewood everyday. We was boys and didn't like work or cold so we built fires under the spruce trees and stood around them. The smoke broke up going through the trees, so no one at the school knew what we was doin'. Ever silly us, eh?"

Although I made a mental note to talk more about school at another time, I pressed on to satisfy my curiosity. "Why did you need to get back to the island in such a hurry? What was the emergency? "

I had a number of suspicions about the emergency, but, not wanting to prolong the preparatory conversation, I didn't ask anything further.

"The Leafs were playin' and my radio died. Now that's an emergency!"

He laughed his staccato laugh, and we talked some more.

The Feast

Every Thanksgiving, my extended family would gather at someone's house for a huge dinner. Cousins who saw each other only once a year felt like they grew up together, because of these meals. Parents and grandparents, aunts and uncles, to whom the cousins belonged, laughed and cried together over life's events rehearsed so often, from year to year, that everyone knew what was coming at the first word of any story. "Tell us about the time that . . ." and "Do you remember when . . ." were phrases heard from the moment the first guest arrived.

New little cousins were introduced to the family with much passing from hand to hand and a great deal of being lifted into the air and dropped a short distance to be caught by the lifter, laughing, "Oops a daisy!" The holiday seemed to give everyone an excuse to stop their busy lives and travel to be with family. Occasional telephone calls and chance meetings at the store sustained familial relationships the rest of the year, but the holiday feast brought the family together, marking the movement of time.

I remember that my Aunt Till, whether she could come to the dinner or not, sent homemade hard candies covered with confectioner's sugar. The sugar always ended up all over my family dinner suit. The delicious candy stuck my teeth together if I tried to chew a piece as it softened in my mouth. My Uncle George and Aunt Virginia, as I remember, always brought spiced pumpkin pie with a bowl of whipped cream for a topping. My grandfather brought his Polaroid, capturing forever either half-stuffed mouths or stiff-smiled family portraits. When dinner was at our house, my mother prepared almost the whole meal.

We all sat around a dining room table that was draped with a beautiful white linen tablecloth held down by gold-rimmed china plates with matching cups and saucers. There were delicate water glasses. Silver forks, spoons, and knives were placed on three sides of the dinner plates, defying everyone but the hostess to unravel the mystery of their use. Every few moments, during the meal, I would look unobtrusively around the table to make sure I had the correct utensil in hand. In the centre of the table, there was usually some kind of flower arrangement flanked on each end with a crystal candlestick and burning candle for atmosphere. Bumping the table not only spilled little bits of water from shaking water goblets, but often caused melted wax from the candles to spatter randomly onto the table.

We always had turkey and candied yams, with a big bowl of creamed corn, a smaller bowl of creamed onions—for my father—, and homemade dinner rolls. Water was poured into the long-stemmed crystal goblets that toppled easily if someone was playing at the table and not paying attention to how to eat properly. Butter and jellied cranberries were served on little crystal plates with little silver serving utensils.

Each major dish was served in a bowl that matched the china plates. The serving bowls were lined up on a wooden sideboard of some kind. The adults often commented that the sideboard was a great focal point for the dining room. The hostess would take a bowl from the sideboard, hand it to the host at the head of the table, and then it would be passed around until it returned to the head of the table to be placed again on the sideboard by the hostess. Each dish, with the exception of the turkey, was an adventure in passing and serving. The most difficult things to pass were the cranberry sauce, which wanted to slide off the little serving plate, and the gravy, served with a ladle that always dripped. The turkey was carved at the table by the head of the house. Each person passed his or her plate to the head of the table, and was asked, "White meat or dark?"

Even as a boy, I was struck by the beauty of the table. The white tablecloth formed a beautiful background for all the colours and shiny reflections. But I also knew that the tablecloth would tell the story of how carefully I had eaten. Every drop of anything that missed plate or mouth showed up on that white expanse after dishes and silverware were removed.

I would hear, "Who was sitting here?"

"Wasn't that where Jimmy was sitting? Yes, right next to Nana."

"Well, he dribbled gravy all over Dorothy's beautiful tablecloth."

"Get some cold water quickly and soak the spot. We don't want it to set."

And so, the passage of time was marked by family dinners. Gradually, one member of the family and then another would be absent from the meal. For some, there would be no more family gatherings. Others were building their own family gatherings far from the security of familiar sideboards. Those who were absent became topics of conversation for those who missed them.

I became one of those absent from the family dinner once I moved to northern Quebec to work for the Anglican Church of Canada in the Cree village of Mistassini. I often thought about those dinners, considering how life was no longer the same for any of us who had gathered around the china and crystal-laden table to enjoy being together.

Evadney, self-appointed village organizer and part-time town crier of Mistassini, seemed to know what everyone was doing or needed to be doing. Just before I officiated at my first wedding, she arrived at my door to discuss village weddings. Evadney was short and plump with a bushy hairdo reminiscent of the fifties in my culture. She wore large, horn-rimmed glasses, giving her the appearance of an owl. Perhaps this is where she got her authority. Evadney always wore a long, flowing cloak rather than a coat or jacket. She had a heavy cloak for the winter and a light, colourful cloak for the summer.

Evadney's energy was boundless and her talking endless. She informed me of how the couples entered the church, where they would stand, and where I was to stand, generally offering advice on everything from which stole I was to wear to how to light the candles. I was simultaneously amused and grateful. When she told me that I had to attend the wedding feast, I was genuinely excited. Here was a chance to attend a family dinner again; not with my family, but it would be nice to be part of a gathering.

The upcoming wedding was somewhat overwhelming for me, so Evadney's information was comforting. Not only was it my first ceremony; six couples were getting married at one time. Multiple weddings in Mistassini were common as a means of sharing expense. If not distantly related, all of the couples had grown up together, so weddings became gatherings of friends and family.

The logistics of the wedding were fairly normal but multiplied times six. Marriage preparation was planned as a group. The rehearsal had as many people in attendance as an average-sized southern wedding. Church furnishings were rearranged to accommodate six couples and their attendants. A large table was placed outside the church where the couples would retire to sign the marriage licenses and parish register. Movement was choreographed to allow the couples, their attendants, and the congregation to receive communion. I stood everyone in alphabetical order in an attempt to reduce the possibility of marrying the wrong man to the wrong woman. Six little boys were taught how to carry little heart-shaped pillows with rings tied to them and when to hold those rings up to be blessed.

On the afternoon of the wedding, I left the rectory to walk the fifty yards to the long, narrow, squared log church. The church was painted white. It sat on a small grassy hill with its front door overlooking beautiful Mistassini Lake. The cross on the steeple was turned a bit to the west so that it would face the small spit of land around which families paddled returning from the winter hunt. The first thing they would see of the village, after surviving the rigours of the winter, was the cross welcoming them home.

The grassy hill was covered with people—hundreds of laughing, talking people. A wave a silence spread through the jubilant crowd as I walked to the church. Inside, people were standing along the walls and sitting everywhere on the floor, because there were no seats left in the hard, wooden pews. Normally, the church held 300 people comfortably. It seemed that over twice that many people were packed into the building. Everyone seated on the floor, in front of the altar rail, had to move so that the couples would have some place to stand with their attendants. I asked the parents of the couples to sit in the cedellia in the sanctuary to be close to the wedding. I had no idea if this was liturgically legal, but it seemed the right thing to do. One of the fathers sat in the Bishop's throne with his three youngest children squirming on his lap. It was a pretty big chair.

Although the couples had some difficulty walking down the aisle full of happy, eager friends and family, the wedding went off without a hitch. Everyone said the repeated parts together. I pronounced each couple married separately. A roar rolled from inside the church to the grass outside as the couples shyly kissed, closing the ceremony. A line of assorted, decorated vehicles was waiting to carry everyone to the wedding supper. After documents were signed, the couples and their attendants left.

I was preparing to take off my robes when the first person out of the church shook my hand, once, firmly. He had put something in my hand. I looked. It was a five-dollar bill. This was strange, but I thanked him. The next person did the same. Almost every person who had attended the wedding, in the church or on the grass, shook my hand, giving me some money. I stuffed the money through my robe into my pockets and inside my belt. As the church emptied and my pockets filled, I began stuffing the bills up my sleeves. I did not know how many people had attended that wedding, but everyone waited to shake my hand in turn and say thank you for the ceremony. It was exhausting in the warmest way possible.

After changing out of my robes, I left the church to walk to the community centre. There was no need to lock the church. In fact, the building did not have a lock. No one would enter the church other than to pray or clean. The walk to the community centre took me down a short hill to a marshy piece of land between two peninsula-like arms of the village. I crossed a long, wooden bridge, recently built to replace a muddy path. Climbing up the hill to the other side of the village, Mistassini Lake stretched as far as I could see, rimmed with a grey-brown ribbon of sand and stone that separated the deep blue of the lake from the multi-hued green of thick forest. Directly in front of me was the tumbledown house of an independent fur trader. The small, abandoned Roman Catholic Church was just up the hill from there. Along the remainder of the peninsula, a single row of log houses pointed to the main part of the village about half a mile to the north. The community centre, where the feast was being held, was almost at the end of that row.

There were cars and trucks of all descriptions parked everywhere, in every direction, at the community centre. This was obviously a much bigger family meal than I had ever attended. A small crowd, standing on the porch in front of battered, double doors, parted. Someone opened the door.

The windowless hall was packed with people. Bare bulbs, placed the length of the ceiling, lighted the massive room. I could barely see the wedding party at a table at the far end. Guests were seated on the floor with a few people standing around each exit. There were so many people that I could not focus on anyone to see who was there. The crowd seemed an indistinguishable mass of coloured scarves and baseball caps. Everyone was there.

Somewhere close by, someone shouted, "*Ayemihaochimaw!*" "The minister!"

The word actually meant "praying boss." *Ayemihao*, the third person singular of the word "to pray," and *ochimaw*, the term used for a leader or boss, were combined: praying boss.

It passed through the crowd, reaching the ears of a woman standing near the wedding table. She began to weave her way through the crowd toward me. It was Evadney. I learned later that she was the acting "*Mokoshanochimashkwao*," or the feast boss woman. I didn't know if she was qualified to run a community feast, but here she was, beckoning to me to follow.

Picking my way through the throng, careful not to step on legs and hands, I noticed that everyone in the building seemed to have a bowl of some description. The adults had large mixing bowls. The children's bowls were smaller. People waved and smiled as I moved by. Although there was a low hum throughout the building, the room was amazingly quiet for having such a huge group of people.

Evadney pointed to the one empty chair at the centre table. "*Api oota.*" "Sit here." The families of the couples were seated on the floor, just in front of the table, around colourful tablecloths of varying patterns. Thoroughly embarrassed to be claiming such a choice spot, I reluctantly, but carefully, moved around the end of the table and took my seat.

At my place was a large paper plate with a picture of two silver wedding bells in the centre. A matching napkin holding plastic cutlery was on the left side of the plate, and a matching pack of matches was at the top. A plastic champagne glass sat on the right. The laughing couples each took a moment to thank me for the wedding. Alfred, who was nicknamed "Jumper" for some reason unknown to me, was sitting on my left. He had pulled the chair out for me, careful not to hit anyone sitting behind the table against the wall.

"It took you long enough to get here. We're starving," he laughed.

Someone further down the table yelled, "Hey, *Ayemihaochimaw*, pray so we can eat!"

I realized that I was to start the feast. Well, it wasn't too different from home. Aside from the fact that the whole village was crammed into one building and sitting on the floor, the feast was going to begin with grace. As I stood, the motion of people turning towards the table rolled through the building. I had brought my prayer book.

"*Ayemihataw!*" I yelled. After reading a grace found in the Cree prayer book, I added a few sentences of thanksgiving for the day and for the couples.

"Amen."

"Amen!" echoed back, and the feast began.

Almost immediately, doors around the hall opened, and women carrying cardboard boxes and aluminum bowls began to pick their way through the crowd. I could not see what was in the boxes, but the women were placing something in the bowl of each guest.

From a door behind the table, Evadney entered, followed by a line of women each with a bowl. Pausing momentarily in front of each person, beginning to my right, she put a piece of goose on each plate. Each woman behind her placed some kind of food on each plate. The stack of food on my plate grew with pieces of goose, slices of turkey white meat, and a thin hose-like substance that I knew to be smoked bear intestine. There were smoked fish and pieces of Kentucky Fried Chicken, lovingly brought the sixty miles from town, along with thin slices of moose meat, and what I thought to be pieces of beaver. My plate was heaping. Mixing bowls throughout the hall were filling.

The women who served used only their hands. At first, this worried me, but then I realized it was an efficient way to serve such a huge meal. Each group of women had a section of the hall to feed. They walked through the crowd with their box or bowl distributing to each person in their section. The hall was a mass of laughing people with five lines of women playing "follow the leader."

No one seemed to be eating. Some children were nibbling, but most people were talking with those sitting around them or teasing the women who were serving. Even the newlyweds were talking and laughing or calling to family members on the floor in front of them. They weren't eating. Not wanting to be rude or different, I resisted temptation and refrained from eating despite being hungry.

I was brought back to my plate as someone put a chunk of bannock on top of the meat. Bannock is a scone-type bread introduced to the Crees by the Hudson's Bay Company a century before. It is baked in a pan or on a stick over an open fire. After several pieces of bannock had been placed on my pile, slices of steamed pudding were brought. "Poodin" is a mixture of flour and raisins steamed in cheesecloth. Molasses is added for sweetness, giving it a dark look and rich taste. With the poodin on top of the pile, I thought the food supply must be exhausted. I was wrong. A woman came by with a huge bowl of mashed potatoes. While I was wondering where this should go, she plunked a spoonful on top the bannock. Next came a lady with some kind of yellowy gravy. Before I could ask what it was, it was plopped next to the mashed potatoes.

Jumper leaned over and whispered: "Bear grease."

When I gave him what must have been a questioning look, he continued.

"It's for the meat. Take a piece of meat and put some fat on it, like this."

He cut a piece of moose meat, scooped a little bear grease onto it with his plastic knife, and ate it.

"It's good. Try it!"

I did. It was good.

Evadney appeared, holding an empty box. "You don't eat here," she informed me. "Everyone takes it home for another time. They have food to eat for a while. You will like it."

"Nice wedding," she commented, shaking my hand. Before reaching to shake Jumper's hand, beginning the trek down the table greeting each couple, she handed me a piece of tinfoil from her empty-looking box.

"Cover your food with this," she suggested.

She gave each person at the table a piece of tinfoil. Most people in the hall had towels of some kind to cover their bowls. A few had tinfoil, but all had come prepared to carry their food home.

As Evadney moved down the table, a general stir ran throughout the hall. Family members in front of the table formed a line and began shaking hands with each newlywed. The stir around the hall turned into a low rumble as everyone got to their feet, joining the line at the table. The greeting that ended the feast was arm-numbing, but fun. Young and old passed along the table, balancing bowls and plates long enough to shake each person's hand. Smiles were limitless. "Thank you's" in both Cree and English were genuine.

Exhausted, but happy, I left the hall, pausing a moment to breathe in the cool evening air and look at the lake. The glitter and formality of family dinners fondly remembered was missing. I had never seen people serve with their bare hands. My family did not serve mashed potatoes on top of the dinner rolls. Somehow, for all these years, we had forgotten the bear grease altogether. But the joy of the crowd, at my first Cree feast, was like the joy I felt when the first guest arrived for Thanksgiving dinner at home. It was multiplied by 1,000 happy hearts.

As I stood thinking and gazing, Evadney found her way to me once again. She smiled and looked at me through her large glasses.

"Feasts are always good, because we share."

One Man's Mile

There are few passions in life that capture a person like fishing. Fishing stimulates all of the senses at the same time. From the moment of decision to go fishing until the last mouthful of a meal fresh caught, from anticipation to fulfillment, fishing is a total life experience. Fishing can be energetic or relaxing, easy or dangerous. It can be as simple as throwing bait and bobber off a dock or as complicated as trolling with costly boat and downrigger, scanning the depths with a fish finder. Equipment and venue do not change the wonder of the sport.

Fishing is one reason to be outdoors. Thinkers throughout the ages have debated whether a fisherman chooses a place to fish or a species to catch when setting out for a day of angling. Does the fisherman return to the same spot year after year because of results, or situation? While living in northern Quebec, I found that I did not have to consider that question. Every fishing trip brought bounty and beauty.

Perhaps the most captivating form of this pastime is fly-fishing: delivery of an artificial bug to the fish in an enticing way. Fly-fishing requires casting technique, as the line is thrown, not the weight of lure or bait. One needs the ability to read water, utilizing varying depths and currents; and an understanding of the habits of particular species of fish to know how and where to deliver the fly. Fly-fishing is not without its frustrations. It is often easier to lay a fly on the leaf of a tree or a distant bush than right over the swirl of a rising trout. An open area over water full of fish in a beautiful, verdant setting is a fly caster's dream.

Because fish are a major food source for the Crees of northern Quebec, every lake and river is known for its supply. Anyone in a village old enough to talk could tell you what kinds of fish were in which lake. And, if the lake held many different species, most people could tell which bay was best for what kind of fish. It seemed that every lake or river held fish of some kind. But not every lake or river was good for fishing. So, I asked people where to fish when I wanted to try some place new.

Johnny Shaky had come by to visit, so I thought I would ask him about places to fish. Johnny was tall and lean. He was one of those people that looked like he had just gotten out of bed no matter what he wore. A thick mass of long, black hair covering eyes and ears did as it pleased, having avoided combing for some time. Large, brown, calloused hands attested to the fact that Johnny knew about hard work. Johnny had a quick, bright smile and wide eyes that made him look perpetually surprised.

I had asked someone once about Johnny's nickname. Nicknames were common among the Crees. If you had a predominant habit or characteristic or had made a huge mistake of some kind at some point in your life, the Crees gave you a nickname. Usually the reason for the name was obvious. I had never seen Johnny shake, so I wondered about the name. Someone told me that the name had grown out of an uncontrollable excitement over candy as a boy.

As Johnny came into the house, he saw my fly rod by the door and commented on the reel. A fly reel is built only to hold line, not to assist in casting. I explained to Johnny why the rod was so long and thin and the reel so round and thick. Either Johnny understood from my brief description of how trees, brush, and wind could complicate fly casting, or he had some knowledge of fly-fishing in the area.

"There is a good lake for that fishing a mile from the creek at the end of Quiet Bay," he offered. "No wind, no trees, and good trout."

"Could I find it pretty easily?"

I was immediately excited. I could have asked Johnny to take me to the lake, but things were not done that directly. He knew I would need help finding the place, so if he wanted to go, he would volunteer.

"Maybe." Johnny sounded dubious about my ability to find the lake. "I could take you."

There were two things that I did not know about Johnny that would make our fishing trip interesting: He had incredible stamina, as did most hunters in the north; and he could not see at night.

We set out late the next morning. There was a two-mile paddle to the trail that led to the fly-fishing lake. The morning was bright and clear. Although we had started out late, steam still rose from the stillness of the lake's surface, shrouding the shore in filmy mystery. A canoe is a wonderful way to travel at any time, but on a calm morning, the silent slide punctuated by the dip of paddles brings an almost hypnotic peace. Occasionally, a loon would call, giving proof that the scene was surreal.

Paddling a canoe anywhere with a Cree is not a leisurely experience. When I was a boy on vacation with my family, I would see the beautiful fields and forest pass by and wonder what they hid. I would look at the tall buildings as we crossed cities and think about the people working inside while I was on vacation. I was always an observer because we travelled to get to a destination and did not stop once the trip began until it ended, except for gas or food. Paddling with the Crees was much the same experience. They appreciated the beauty around them—it was their home. But a canoe trip was a means to get somewhere to do something. Once the trip began, paddling was strong and constant until the trip was over or rest was needed.

Johnny and I put my fly rod and a backpack of supplies for the day in the canoe and began the short journey. There was no talking as we cut the glassy lake. Johnny was in the stern steering the canoe. I was in front paddling. Often, the Crees put the novice in the stern, while the experienced person reads the water and guides the canoe. It was assumed that the stern would follow the bow, so the more experienced person read the water. On this trip, Johnny needed to turn at exactly the right spot on the shore, so he drove.

By the time Johnny turned toward shore, my right side was beginning to numb. Johnny manoeuvred us to a sandy beach next to a small creek. To him, the little creek was a street sign for the road to the little lake. We climbed out of the canoe and pulled it up onto the bank. Once the few pieces of equipment we had brought were on our backs, we set off up a small trail. We could leave the canoe as it sat, paddles and all, with no fear of theft. Should someone see it, he or she would simply note the spot and pass on, honouring our need to return home.

Beginning our hike following the creek, Johnny announced, "The lake is a mile."

Crees set a stiff, constant pace on foot as well as in a canoe. Years of portaging through the forest, carrying canoe and gear over trails from one lake to another, had produced a rhythm that every member of the village copied when on the trail. At the pace that Johnny set, I would soon be fly-fishing.

We began walking at the mouth of a small river at the end of a small bay on the huge inland lake. Looking across the little bay ringed by black spruce reflecting off still water was like looking at a postcard. The trees began about seventy-five yards from the bank, which to that point was covered with thick, tall grass, green and straight except where crushed down by some animal's run to the water to drink. I was struck by the fact that the human trail was tiny and used only occasionally as the first portage on a journey inland from the lake.

The grass ring around the bay looked almost manicured for its uniformity. Spring thaw flooding from the creek made the growth of trees impossible.

We walked along the creek to the woods. The trail turned right, away from the creek. Actually the trail turned south. Walking up the creek, we were walking east into the sun. Turning right put the sun on our left shoulders, so we were walking generally south. I had gotten into the habit of memorizing landmarks and watching the position of the sun to note direction. Normally I carried a compass, but I didn't need one on this short hike with Johnny as a guide.

Once in the trees, following the trail wasn't difficult. The spruce forest was thick. Trees laden with "old man's beard," thick, stringy, grey moss covering lower branches, absorbed noise, breeze, and much of the sunshine. Johnny knew the way, so we carried on confidently.

We walked silently for the most part. The quiet was being punctuated by the occasional muttered "Rabbit," or "Martin," as Johnny identified animal trails for me. Sometimes, he would just point, and I would stare in the general direction to find a porcupine in a tree or a hawk soaring in a blue hole above in the trees. After what seemed a long time, we found ourselves in a meadow. A drummond—a rounded ridge of rock and earth deposited or carved by an ancient glacier—ran in front of us.

"Now we follow this hill."

I was imagining the rhythm of my cast. I could see the trout rising to my fly. I could almost feel the jerky pull of the fight.

The trail was more evident here in the grass. Apparently, this part had been used more, because a dirt path of brown cut the green of the meadow. I guess I had missed an intersection somewhere behind us. The rounded ridge was to our left, so on the way back, it would be to our right. That was simple.

Johnny paused. I could hear the silence. There was nothing but the call of a bird now and again to cut the stillness. Johnny sat down on a log. He took off his backpack. We both had backpacks with drinks and sandwiches. I had my flies, an extra spool of line, and my rod, broken down in sections. I glanced at my watch. We had been walking almost two hours.

"Let's eat! We're almost there," said Johnny.

"Why not eat when we get to the lake?"

I thought I might be able to fish and eat intermittently. We had to be close. We had walked at a good pace for surely more than a mile.

"We eat when we eat and fish after." This was practical, but frustrating. Sitting on the soft grass with my back to the big log, I took out a sandwich and a bottle of water.

"How often have you been to this little lake?" I asked simply because I wanted to make conversation.

"My brother told me about it. He fishes."

To a Cree man, describing how to get to a little lake somewhere in the forest was as easy as a city dweller giving directions to the store or the post office. "Go to the end of the bay. Get out of the canoe at the big rock shaped like a loon. Walk toward the hill until you see a dead spruce taller than all the rest." These were bush directions. Johnny knew how to get to the lake. I wasn't worried about getting lost. I was thinking that I actually had no first-hand knowledge of the lake— either the fish population, or the "castability" of the lake.

"No bugs in the bush," Johnny observed. "At least not today."

Having spent some time walking through the forest covered with blackflies or mosquitoes, I was thankful for the airy buglessness.

"I know. Why is that, today?"

"Too hot."

Johnny was moving before I realized he had finished eating.

Picking up my leftovers and throwing them into the backpack, I shouted every child's question, "How much farther?"

"Not far now."

It was the "now" that I heard. We had already walked a long way at a good, tiring pace. I had thought we were not far when stepping out of the canoe.

The meadow began to change as the long grass gave way to small hillocks of tea plant and low bush cranberries. We were on a trail through an old bog. Bogs are lakes that have been reclaimed by moss. The filmy moss grows—as does sod—over the years, encroaching on the lake while forming a fairly solid, spongy, ever-widening carpet where the shores once were, until the lake is covered. Although old moss can be walked on, a trail is a good idea because there are often holes in the covering where the lake has won.

I saw the lake ahead—perhaps a four-acre pond. Johnny followed the path halfway around the lake to a sandy spot on the shoreline. This little pond, its shore lined with moss, was all I had hoped it would be. We must have been standing on what had been an island before the moss began its inexorable growth. Behind the rocky sand of the shore where we stood was more firm moss. There were no trees or bushes behind, and there was wide, open, still water in front; a fly caster's dream. Small rings dotted the pond's surface as insects hit the water, succumbing to the heat of the day. They were gobbled up by rising trout.

I chose a tiny dry fly, a white miller, with a number fourteen hook. A dry fly floats if presented properly. A wet fly is designed to sink. With each cast, a trout rose to the fly. Timing is an essential part of fishing with a dry fly. The fish does not hook itself. The fisherman must hook the fish at exactly the right moment. I missed quite a few and caught quite a few. The trout were not big, but they were fun: brook trout between eight and twelve inches long, a nice challenge on a light fly rod.

What a wonderful afternoon it turned out to be. Johnny tried his hand at fly casting. A fly rod is not whipped on the down swing of the cast like a spinning or bait-casting rod. Rather, the fly line is thrown back, and the backward momentum used to carry the line into the forward throw. The rod tip is always held high. Because the fly weighs nothing, the fly line itself is thrown. This lake was the perfect place to learn. Unless Johnny let the fly drop in the moss, he could not get caught in anything. He caught a number of trout. We cleaned what trout we kept, packed our gear, and started home. The sun was low. We had stayed perhaps too long.

Once around the lake and out of the moss meadow, we came to the path through the grass. It was dusk. We had stayed too long. Johnny slowed and stopped. From a few steps behind, I saw Johnny motion me ahead. I moved by him only to feel him grab my shirt.

"Bad eyes," he admitted quietly. "I can't see after the sun goes down."

The implications of this admission were overwhelming. We had almost a three-hour walk. We had almost a three-hour walk in the dark. We had almost a three-hour walk in the dark through countryside I did not know. We had almost a three-hour walk in the dark through countryside I did not know with a guide that couldn't see. And we had no compass.

Johnny sensed my uneasiness. "Just walk back the way we came."

"You really can't see anything once it begins to get dark?"

This was a stupid question. Once I thought about it, I realized it came out of my fear, which stemmed from the fact that I couldn't see anything after dark either—because, after all, it was dark. Somehow, although I had never really thought about it before, the men that I had hunted with didn't worry about being in the dark. They were able to travel at night. In fact, apparently, it was easier to hunt a moose at night when only a hulking shadow could be seen.

With dark approaching, I found that night hunting was not one of Johnny's skills.

"Just walk on the path," Johnny advised, not sounding worried at all.

I could still see the path, so I began to walk. Realizing that I could feel the difference between the path and the grass next to it, I gained some confidence. When I got off the path, the tall grass rubbed my ankles and the ground was a bit softer. I walked as fast as I could, attempting to take advantage of what light we had. Johnny was right behind me. We didn't talk much.

The thickening night was clear without a hint of clouds or fog. Although the rising moon was waning, it was still large. My hope rose with it. The drummond became a shadowy mass off to one side. I realized that, even if not on the path, as long as the drummond stayed where it was, we were okay. To keep panic at bay, I tried not to think about what we were doing. With feet on the path and eyes on the shadow, our progress was better than expected.

Eventually, there was another mass in front of us. I could see that we were approaching something but couldn't make it out. So far, with the moon, the grass, and the drummond, things had gone pretty well. My confidence followed the moon's example, gradually waning, as I saw that we had crossed the meadow and were on the edge of the spruce trees. My guess was that we had been walking for about an hour and a half. Johnny had walked at a quick pace coming. We were going much more slowly now, for obvious reasons.

In the moonlight, the trees made a solid wall, with shadows filling gaps where branches failed to overlap. We would have to become like the ghosts in movies, dematerializing to step through the wall.

"Johnny, do you know the trail? I can't see anything now that we are at the trees."

I didn't whine the question but attempted to temper my voice with a masculine concern.

Johnny answered with masculine lack of concern.

"Sure I know it, but I can't see. Just walk and feel until you can see."

I stepped straight ahead where the trail went into the forest. Taking Johnny's advice, I paid attention to what was on the trail. It was hard packed and somewhat concave. Experimenting before moving too far from the meadow, I ventured right and then left. Surprisingly, I could feel needles and branches on the forest floor as soon as I got off the trail. Stepping back on to the trail provided the comfort of a smooth, concave surface.

Johnny was holding tightly to my belt, matching me step for step.

"Slow is okay. Just stay on the trail."

The predominant sound, when we weren't talking, was silence. In the distance, an occasional loon call broke the silence.

"The lake," Johnny observed.

"I guess so," I concurred. "Now if that loon will only call every two minutes for the next hour or so we should be okay."

"He won't," Johnny observed.

I continued my forward progress, speeding up a bit as I gained confidence. A step off the trail brought the crackling of dried twigs, the bristly slap of spruce boughs, and often a trip over the trail edge. Coming back to the trail, Johnny would affirm my course correction with a monosyllabic, "Good!"

After awhile, I realized that the path through the forest was straight. This was logical. Turning a corner on a narrow trail bordered by a wall of trees while carrying a canoe would not be easy. So the trail was straight. Suddenly, I had a flash of Miss Thorpe's 8th grade geometry class. She had told us we would always need geometry. I thought geometry only related to shooting pool, but now realized that the axiom, "The shortest distance between two points . . ." buoyed my spirits.

As I calmed down, realizing that we could make our way on the forest trail, I began to hear other night sounds. The scurry of small creatures running before us seemed a loud scrapping in the silence. At one point, the call of an owl was comforting in an eerie kind of way.

"*Ohomishoo*," Johnny announced.

The silence that followed the owl's call emphasized the appropriateness of the onomatopoetic name for the bird of the night.

I was calculating that we had come about halfway across the spruce forest when I experienced a phenomenon that can frighten even an experienced forest traveller at night. I heard something walking just off the trail to my right. Johnny had offered one-word commentaries on things around me all day, so I expected him to comment on what might be accompanying us. He said nothing.

The footsteps were clear, but there was no crackling of brush. I paused for a moment as if catching my breath. Johnny stopped. So did our companion. As

I began to walk again, I walked faster. The footsteps off the trail kept pace. I had heard bears move through the bush; they sounded like bulldozers. A moose would never follow like this. This was large, but quiet and curious enough to keep pace. Or maybe hungry enough to keep pace.

The combination of the darkness, an unseen trail, and silence was bringing me to the edge of panic, despite having Johnny right behind me. I could wait no longer.

"What is following us, Johnny?"

Johnny smiled a lot but rarely laughed at someone's ideas unless he knew they were intended to be funny. Crees studiously avoided embarrassing others. An idea that struck someone as funny would instantly bring hand to mouth, hiding giggles.

Johnny laughed out loud. "We follow us."

This seemed an odd statement, but I had sense enough not to ask any more questions. With the weight of a laugh and a complete sentence behind his answer, I knew that Johnny knew something I didn't.

We had stopped walking. So had the footsteps. I stomped my feet twice. Two stomps sounded off the trail. Not a little embarrassed, I realized that our companion was an echo. The night's stillness, with the thickness of the trees around us, caught our footfalls and threw them back. Crees may studiously avoid embarrassing others, but I could tell from Johnny's breathing that he was laughing pretty hard as quietly as he could.

Continuing on through this forest nether world, little was said. I had to admit to myself that my reaction to the echo was funny.

"Anything following us now?"

Johnny was quick, "Yes, we still follow us."

It became apparent that one could see quite a bit in the dark once eyes became accustomed. Although we could not see the moon, it did offer light through the trees, creating shadows of objects. We had been walking in the dark shadows a long time. We no longer saw glimpses of the moon through holes in the trees. It had moved a long way, also.

When the senses are not bombarded with things to interpret, there are wonderful subtleties all around that become vividly apparent. We seemed to be walking with more intent, although the pace had changed very little. I was no longer looking around, having become familiar with the feel of the trail. Johnny seemed lost in thought, no longer ejaculating the names of sounds. I became aware of a few things that I had not noticed before.

The fish in my bag had a fishy smell. I didn't know if they were spoiling or if I was just paying attention. I came to the conclusion that this was the way they were supposed to smell.

Although there was no breeze, I could hear the spruce boughs whispering. Often hunters had told me stories of spruce trees telling them where moose were waiting, or that a storm was coming, or where a beaver was living. On this quiet, shadowy path, I had the feeling that the trees were speaking to me, but I did not know the language.

Suddenly, I realized that we were close to the lake. I could not say with certainty how I knew, but there were new subtleties. I was sure I could smell the water. Having spent much of my life by lakes, I must have smelled water before, but I couldn't remember. For me, smells often trigger mental images. This slight smell took me to my childhood on another path after a soft rain, approaching the beach at our summer cottage. We were close.

I could tell that the air pressure had changed. At least something in the space around us, now not occupied by trees, was different. Maybe, as we moved, we were pushing air ahead of us. In the trees, there had been no place to go, so it had built up. Now that we were close to the lake, we were pushing it out over the little bay. Less air was building up in front of us. I didn't think it was good science, but it was a nice thought for lifting the spirits.

The silence was different here. Further back on the path, it had been almost a roar. In the meadow with shadows lengthening, it had been a blanket. Here it was like a cushion. There had been a change. It wasn't exactly silence. I thought I could hear grass rustle. I thought I could here ripples in the water, maybe a muskrat swimming. We were close to the canoe.

Johnny heard and felt the changes also.

"Canoe's just ahead."

I still couldn't see anything but the shadow of the tree wall, so I kept the same pace. Gradually things lightened ahead. Suddenly, the wall on both sides of the trail was gone. The air was open, with a slight breeze. I still could not see anything, but I could hear the slight wash of waves on the shore.

"Find the canoe," Johnny suggested.

I had already begun to walk to the bank. This was difficult, because the tall grass hid the trail and I could not clearly see the creek bank, which, as I remembered, had a drop of about three feet. Johnny let go once we cleared the trees. He walked tentatively to my left away from the creek bank. I stayed

One Man's MILE

close enough to the bank to know that I was walking in the right direction. Johnny stayed close enough to me to know that he was walking in the right direction. The ground began a gradual downward slope. I realized that grass had given way to pebbles and sand. Staring into the night, I saw a mass on the water's edge that was our canoe.

"Here's the canoe, Johnny."

"Good."

We made our way to the canoe, stowed our gear, and prepared to head home. Johnny pushed the canoe into the water so the stern was afloat and climbed in. Once seated, he dug his paddle into the lake bottom to hold the canoe in place for me. I climbed in, knelt in the bow with my rear against the seat, and dug my paddle into the ground, pushing us backwards. I had learned that the seats in a canoe were for resting your back. Kneeling in a canoe keeps the centre of gravity close to the water with less chance of a sudden movement tipping the craft.

As we struck out from shore, it seemed that we travelled on a mirror. I could not see far in any direction, but the lake was as smooth as glass. My eyes had become accustomed to this new shade of darkness. I could see the bank vaguely reflected in the water. We simply had to paddle parallel to the bank to get home.

I was struck by a new sensation as we paddled that canoe.

Our paddles cut the water at the same time. This created a soft splash. Lifting the paddles to stroke again dropped a spray of water along the paddles' path over the water. The canoe lurching forward caused a swish as bow cut water. There was no sound other than the continuous subdued sound of paddles and canoe on water.

There was a slight breeze at our backs, strong enough to feel but too soft to disturb the water. We had felt the breeze as we reached the bank from the woods. Once underway, because our forward speed matched that of the breeze at our backs, we no longer felt any sensation of movement. Because of the murky darkness, it was difficult to tell shore from lake from sky. It seemed that we were suspended, arms moving paddles, but sight, hearing, and the sensation of motion had been eliminated. I felt completely peaceful.

"There's the village," Johnny announced.

I was almost asleep—or almost hypnotized—and paddling by rote. I could see small points of light in the distance. It occurred to me that we had not talked once about the fishing since beginning our trek to the canoe.

"It was a long day, but worth it."

I expected an answer, even though this statement seemed fairly complete in and of itself. Johnny said nothing.

"The fly-fishing was just great in that little lake." Again, I stated the obvious. There was no need for a reply.

I caught on. To engage someone else in a conversation, one had to leave room for someone else to make a reply.

"Do you think I could find that lake again by myself?"

"Yes, in the daylight," Johnny responded in the fledgling conversation.

"I know we took a long time to walk back in the dark, but we walked a lot farther than a mile," I observed.

Johnny thought for a moment. I supposed my observation seemed reasonable, but then his brother had told him the lake was a mile from the beach. Faced with choosing between his brother's statement of distance and my observation from recent experience, Johnny responded in the only way he could.

"One man's mile is different from another man's mile."

The Coat

Hattie lived between the sandy shores of beautiful Lake Mistassini and the vast boreal forest of northern Quebec. It seemed to me that I had never seen her standing. I always saw her in a camp, sitting in a corner of her tent working on something or other. Although the village of Mistassini consisted of neat rows of small, one-storey log homes, most of the older people preferred living in tents or log lodges in the bush, using their houses as large storage sheds. Hattie was no exception. In the winter, she lived with her sons and their families in a traditional Cree winter lodge 200 miles from the village. In the summer, she stayed about a mile from the village in a tent along the one dirt road leading to or from the south, depending on your point of view. Signs of the seasons, snow and ice, wind and rain, sun and heat, bugs and smells and whispering trees decorated Hattie's home.

Hattie was small, standing or seated. Her oval face was lined from smiling and brown from her life in the bush. Her eyes were dark and observant. Her silver hair was neatly pulled back in a bun, never out of place regardless of the task at hand. She always wore a brightly coloured dress over dark pants, with a sweater of some kind. Although she sat with her legs folded back, sometimes one leg would straighten, revealing a moccasin that disappeared into her pant leg. Hattie looked to me like she would feel chilly in a lodge in the winter, and sweltering in the summer, but her dress never varied. She also looked like her legs would ache from sitting on them, but she never stood while I was with her.

Hattie worked at all kinds of things in her corner. Sometimes she occupied herself with sewing, her material and thread covering a blanket spread out on the spruce bough floor within arm's length. Sometimes she laced snowshoes, pulling hand-cut moosehide string from a huge ball that rolled around on a piece of cardboard on the floor next to her. At times, her lap draped in clear plastic, Hattie helped clean small game or cut up moose meat for the pot. Hattie had never been to a southern town. She could not be separated from her culture or the forest upon which it thrived.

Henry came to Mistassini from a southern town, not to teach or tell, but to watch and learn. Somewhat of a misfit in his own New Hampshire culture, he had developed an affinity with native North Americans through articles and pictures. Forays into villages accessible from his home opened his eyes to many native technologies for living that were gradually disappearing as the chain of oral tradition was broken. Henry instinctively knew that the process of building a birchbark canoe should not be lost to the ease of moulding fibreglass. He understood that the beauty and practicability of handmade moosehide moccasins should not disappear in shipments of rubber boots.

Crees had for generations, as do all people, integrated into their lives things from other cultures to make life easier without compromising cultural boundaries. The snowmobile, outboard motor, tin wood stove, and rifle were all accepted as useful imports from southern life. Henry hoped to save some parts of native culture through the use of modern technology. His life's ambition became videotaping traditional crafts and technologies, preserving them for the future. Henry valued native crafts, but being a product of his own culture, often did not understand the craftsman.

Customs and language are obvious areas where cultural misunderstandings can occur. But subtleties of values, time, and relationship often build parallel paths of life that may never intersect. Good intentions across cultural barriers can be interpreted as condescension or colonialism at worst, and silliness at best. The Crees of northern Ontario and Quebec, admirably forbearing in their patience with inept, non-native attempts to modernize, evangelize, hospitalize, industrialize, legalize, and categorize, often spent much time laughing and talking about the quirks of a doctor or teacher. Their patience, far greater than that of many who intruded into their culture, grew from the value placed on each individual. A teacher, although funny in appearance and irrelevant in content, was offering something personal and was not to be taken lightly.

Henry was such a person. He was viewed with great interest because of his knowledge of native crafts, but seen as comical because of the funny things he did. He put something that looked like sawdust called "wheat germ" in his bannock. He put a huge piece of plastic across the top of his tent. He usually put the branches in his spruce bough floor upside down. He was quiet when he visited, but gulped his tea and then asked for a second cup. He was interesting and amusing. People liked to see him arrive in Mistassini.

Age had a place of honour in all the tents and houses of Mistassini. Family history, information about trapping grounds, religious tradition, characteristics of animals, and secrets of the bush were passed down by the old people. Each matriarch or patriarch did his or her part, as did Hattie, to help with family chores, passing on what it was to be Cree by teaching traditional skills and telling stories.

Hattie had learned a special skill, as a girl, by watching her grandmother and mother as they worked. She could weave things from rabbit skin: hats, blankets and coats, all used by children for warmth. She had learned how to prepare the skins and how to weave them for maximum warmth. Very few women had learned the skill and even fewer practised it.

Henry was in Mistassini to document snowshoe making. Having heard of Hattie from people in the village, he decided to meet her and film her working with rabbit skin if she were agreeable. Henry had asked me to introduce him to Hattie, assuming that any distrust of strangers would be somewhat dispelled if in the company of the Anglican minister. I could see no harm in taking Henry to see Hattie. On the contrary, I thought that recording her skill was a good idea. More people than Hattie's family would be able to spend some time with this unique woman.

It was spring. Hattie was close to the village. Henry, knowing that winter's grip on the countryside was broken, had travelled north to begin his work. Henry wanted to be near the village for accessibility to the traditional crafts. He pitched his tent within sight of the village on a flat piece of ground only a dozen yards from the lake. The tent with its small, tin, wood stove and white man's version of the spruce bough floor would become Henry's home until early fall when he would be pushed by Arctic air back to his southern home to edit and market his documentaries. Henry's tent was a comfortable place in which to live and plan. His small, red truck with its home-built, red bed cap was his warehouse. My basement provided warmth and power for his battery packs.

As a southern suburbanite, immersed in nature for the first time, I had become aware of the seasons as never before. I looked forward to each change in the world around me as a new treat for the senses. Hattie loved each season because they were her home. She stayed away from the village to be close to the seasons in the bush. Henry enjoyed seasonal changes as much as I did, but made sure that he was not in northern Quebec, where winter was at its coldest.

Each season transformed the landscape and all its inhabitants, bringing beauty and difficulty. The beauty of a snow-draped winter landscape belied the dangers of extreme cold when travelling, and the work necessary to heat house or tent. Summer brought the warmth of relaxation, with hordes of biting insects. Fall gave dramatic splashes of yellows and reds mixed with the evergreens, but also an instinctive urgency to prepare for the coming cold.

Springtime in northern Quebec was a time of joy and expectation for the Crees. The days were long and bright, in contrast to twenty hours daily of winter darkness. Spruce trees seemed to lift their boughs in praise to the sun after months of carrying the burden of snow. Rivers and streams, happy to be free of their icy blanket, climbed over banks as if stretching in the growing warmth. Geese, on the wing, called the way to those behind, in their flight to familiar Arctic nurseries. The hibernators of the north staggered out of dens, gaunt and stiff, to search for the bounty of earth reborn. Adults and children alike unconsciously recognized all these signs of spring and their spirits lifted.

Only the ice and snow seemed angry at the thaw. Ice-plugged culverts under the road, refusing to give way to growing streams, forced tumbling water over low spots, eventually cutting impassible crevices in the dirt. Snow suddenly refused to accept feet on paths that had been solid and welcoming all winter. It allowed unwary walkers to sink, with one leg or both, up to knee or hip, with no handhold for pulling oneself back to the solid path.

Ice, on lakes, having provided everything from hockey arena to highway, suddenly played tricks on the unwary traveller. Appearing solid on the surface, it hid a weakened, honeycombed structure between air and water that gave way when animal or human trusted its weight to this fickle element.

In the spring, Cree hunters and their families moved about their hunting territory, abandoning the log lodges of winter for the mobile canvas cabin tents that could be transported easily and pitched quickly. Eventually, they moved back to the village to spend time with friends and relatives sorely missed over the winter months of hunting in isolation. Hattie combined both enterprises into one move. She left the winter lodge where she had been enjoying the activities of a hunting family and moved to a tent, just off the road, in a wooded glen a mile or so from the village. She was in her beloved forest, but she could witness the comings and goings of the village. She was easily accessible to those who wanted to visit.

One day, Henry and I drove out to Hattie's camp, in the little red truck, so that he could meet her and talk about her skill with rabbit skins. Henry was talkative but focused during the drive. The only discussion was on how best to broach the subject of making a rabbit skin coat with Hattie. He also rehearsed his plans for filming. I could not get to know Henry. He talked only of his work.

Hattie's tent was pitched on a small rise just off the road among some tiny spruce trees that had grown up through debris slashed from under a hydro line. Her tent was small, held in shape by lines tied to large logs laid on packed-down snow. The ground was still too frozen to use tent stakes. A thin stovepipe poked through the front of the tent and turned upward. The top of the tent was grey and black in spots, mildewed from being packed and transported while still wet. The tent flap was open and inviting, hanging to one side of the door, which was held open by the weight of a stick attached across its middle.

Ducking through the door, we found that we had to stoop once inside. I realized the lines, attached to the logs, pulled the walls out, holding the tent at its full width. But they also pulled down the sides. Tall stakes would have pulled out and up. The tent was considerably shorter than intended when it was made, but the height of the tent didn't matter to Hattie. Not only was she short, she was seated most of the time. As we entered the tent, she was seated on a blanket in the far corner to the left of the door. She was stitching something. I thought it was a moccasin. Her granddaughter was seated just next to her, working on what must have been the other half of the pair.

"Whacheyaa," I said once inside, having quickly decided to use no names, because I could not remember the granddaughter's name. Hattie just smiled and raised a hand.

Her granddaughter giggled, saying simply, "Hi!"

I had intended to speak Cree to Hattie but was happy to see that there was someone to translate. "Ni paachiwapamitinan" "We've come to see you," I said a bit tentatively.

Hattie responded simply: "Ma."

All cultures have exclamations that are noises with meaning. In Cree, "Ma" is the equivalent of saying, "You don't say." "Sa" equals "I can't believe it!" or "That's amazing!" "Ka" is more negative: "You have got to be kidding!" Each exclamation was breathed differently, and each transmitted emotion. Hattie was pleased that we had come, but was waiting to find out the purpose of our visit before offering a greeting.

I spoke to Hattie through her granddaughter.

"This is my friend Henry," I began timidly, not sure about what I would say next. "He has come to Mistassini to watch people do different things."

I had decided to start the conversation in a very general way, but it was clear from the looks that I got from both Hattie and her granddaughter that "different things" had brought different things to mind than I had intended.

"Ma," Hattie breathed, making that small sound a three-syllable word.

"Henry would like to watch you make a rabbit skin coat." I decided to drop the subtleties.

"I am not making a rabbit coat. I am making moccasins," Hattie responded frankly.

And so it went for a few sentences.

"Yes, I see you are making moccasins, but we thought you might be able to make a rabbit skin coat when the moccasins are finished."

"I will not be done today," Hattie informed us.

I laughed and told Hattie that we did not want her to make the coat just then, but whenever she had time over the summer.

Hattie informed us of the obvious—at least obvious to anyone who knows fur: "Rabbit coats are made in the fall. The fur is better than now in the spring."

Hattie was missing the basic point of the conversation. Henry was not interested in the coat, but in her *ability* to make the coat. Various approaches to the subject were countered over the next few moments. I knew that Hattie would not want to embarrass a visitor, but it seemed that she was having some fun. Possibly more information would be helpful.

"Henry wants to make sure that people remember how to make rabbit skin coats," I explained in growing detail. "He wants to make a movie of you making a coat. People will watch it in the future."

Hattie's granddaughter seemed to be doing a good job translating, but she kept her eyes down, embarrassed by what she was being asked to say. I still could not remember her name, and did not want to reveal that I had forgotten it.

Looking from one of us to the other, Hattie seemed to ignore the thought that people would watch her make coats. "If someone needs a coat, I can make it for them." She parried our request again, laying out the only valid requirement for her work—need.

"Yes, but people would learn from the movie of you many years from now."

"Ma." Hattie quietly exclaimed. There could be no translation.

Hattie had seen the point. She did not seem particularly enthusiastic, but neither did she attempt to sidestep the issue of making the coat. She continued to sew the moccasin. I noticed that she had not shifted position since we had arrived. Henry and I were seated cross-legged on the floor. Both my legs and back were beginning to hurt. Hattie was fine. Her granddaughter had stopped sewing to concentrate on translating.

I took a moment to glance around the interior of the tent. The wood stove sat on a cement block laid on its side. The bottom of the stove was buckled from fires that were too hot. Next to the stove was a shelf made of a board nailed on top of four stakes driven into the ground. Obviously, the ground had thawed inside the tent. Mildew on the tent was evident from inside, but the interior was still bright and cheery. The spruce bough floor was bare in spots, needing to be replaced. Rolled blankets and neatly stacked clothes were placed in orderly piles along the back wall of the tent. Large pieces of cardboard, of varying heights, lined the bottom of the tent walls except directly behind the stove. These must have been broken-down boxes from the Hudson's Bay Store. I guessed that when someone sat close to the wall, they served to keep the cold off.

Hattie spoke softly, looking at her granddaughter.

"If you bring the child here on Monday, my grandmother says she will make the coat."

Although it was obvious that, in a few seconds of silence, Hattie had considered our request and agreed, we were left off-balance by her answer.

"What child?" I asked, confused and tongue-tied.

Without translating for her grandmother, our translator responded, "The child the coat is for."

I finally asked our translator her name. It seemed right, since she was doing all the work. She was Mary. I explained to her that there was no child that actually needed a coat. Henry just wanted to film her grandmother making a coat. He would keep the coat.

"Ma." Mary understood.

Unfortunately, she translated only the last part of my explanation.

Hattie, with her hand over her mouth hiding her giggle, replied, "That man is too big. It would take too many rabbit skins. He is too old to wear a rabbit coat."

"The coat is not for me to wear," Henry explained, jumping into the conversation for the first time.

"Then why do you want it?" Hattie asked with some suspicion.

Henry, in an attempt to explain his intentions, committed a major tactical error. "Well, I don't really want the coat. I want to film you as you make the coat from beginning to end."

"You want to watch me make a coat that you don't want? I do not have enough rabbit skins to make a coat for you."

Henry thought he would try to counter Hattie with some logic. "Since it's not for me, you can make a small coat."

But Hattie was too quick. "Bring a child the size of the coat you want."

"The size doesn't matter, just make the coat any size." This seemed reasonable to Henry, but I could see that Mary had downcast eyes again so I knew there was a problem.

"I cannot make a coat for no one."

"Do you have a small grandchild?" asked Henry, thinking quickly.

"Yes."

"Could you make a coat for one of them?" Henry had had a "Ma!" experience and quickly decided to solve the pattern problem. Hattie would probably be happy to make a coat for one of her grandchildren.

But Hattie instinctively sidestepped this suggestion. "They don't need coats."

"You could make a coat for one of your grandchildren and then they would have an extra one."

"Sa! How big a coat do you want me to make?"

"It doesn't matter. I just want to film what you do. You do the same thing to make any sized coat, don't you?"

Hattie obviously said something that Mary felt should not be translated, because she began to refer to her grandmother in the third person.

"She says that the bigger the coat, the more there is to do."

Henry, relieved that the issue had moved from making the coat to the size of the coat, answered quickly.

"Maybe it would be good to have you make a coat for the biggest grandchild."

"I don't have enough rabbits."

Henry was beginning to get frustrated. "You can make the coat for the grandchild that will use the rabbits you have."

Again, Hattie spoke softly to her granddaughter.

"My grandmother will pick one. If you come back on Monday, she will be ready to start."

Henry got a bit braver. "May I film you skinning some rabbits?"

Mary spoke in the third person again, so I knew she was concerned about the direction of the conversation. "She does not need any more skins."

"I want to film the whole process, if that is okay. Could I film her skinning some rabbits?" Henry's enthusiasm and focus had returned.

Mary translated, and Hattie smiled, "If there are rabbits, I will skin them."

Although she hadn't directly answered the question, Henry was satisfied.

After conferring quickly, we decided to return on Monday morning to begin filming. Henry just wanted to get started. He could film the process of skinning the rabbits and preparing the skins anytime. The whole time with Hattie had been spent talking about whether or not a coat would be made. I could only imagine the conversation about the cost of the coat. Although she had conceded, Hattie could not understand why anyone would want a coat made when it was not needed. Nor did she understand fully what it meant for her skill to be documented.

"Mary, please tell your grandmother that we will come back on Monday morning. Did your grandmother want to tell us anything more before we go?"

Hattie had said something at the end of Mary's translation while gesturing towards us.

Mary shrugged, considered what to say for a moment, and replied.

"My grandmother said that white men always want something they don't need."

Getting Water

Mistassini Lake, in northern Quebec, is over 130 miles long and almost thirty-five miles wide. A line of islands runs down the centre of the lake, providing haven from the wind for weary boaters and habitat for pike, pickerel, and speckled and lake trout. About halfway up the northwest shore of the lake are the headwaters of the great Rupert River. From Mistassini, the Rupert flows over 300 miles to the James Bay. Two-thirds of the way to the James Bay, the river boils and churns through one of the most spectacular series of rapids in the world.

A drop in elevation of 600 feet over about a mile sends the river crashing against rock and shore, creating awe-inspiring geysers and cascades of foam and froth. Approaching the rapids in a canoe, it is easy to think of continuously rolling thunder heard from miles away. Within a hundred yards of this wonder, yelling voices can't be heard more than a few feet away. Spray from the force of water on rock towers seventy-five feet in the air, topped by a wind-carried mist. It is hard to know sometimes where the sky begins and the cascade ends.

Point of view often determines how something is seen in life. Different people will see the same thing differently, depending on their perspective. No one would even consider attempting to shoot the smallest of swirls in this colossal fountain as he or she viewed the power of it from the bank. Flying low over the rapids in a small plane provided a view of rolling white foam and mist appearing in the blue river and disappearing just as quickly into the quiet flow below. From the window of a commercial airliner with a view of a third of the continent, a curious passenger might see a break of white in a long, unending ribbon of blue.

Different people valued the river for different reasons. Anyone portaging around this falling deluge is in awe of the continuous force of falling water. Cree hunters, since the beginning of time, have honoured the Rupert River rapids as a symbol of nature's power. The fortunate adventurer standing in the falling mist of the cascade marvels at personal insignificance. A naturalist may see an intricately beautiful ecosystem supporting the mighty moose and the fragile arctic lichen. A representative of a Quebec utility would see an inexhaustible source of hydroelectric power and unimaginable wealth.

Annie was eighty-four, a stout, grey-haired granny constantly puffing on an old corncob pipe. She loved life in the bush. She had crawled up the ramp into a single-engine Otter aircraft to be carried from her village on Mistassini Lake into the forest of northern Quebec for the winter.

Annie's entire life was connected to the Rupert River. All the creeks and small rivers on her father's hunting territory ran to the Rupert. The river had been the fall highway to the hunting camp. Because Annie had many relatives in Rupert's House, a village on the James Bay Coast at the mouth of the river, she had come to the portage by the rapids several times, going to visit family. When she married, she hunted with her new husband's family further up the river still, travelling its familiar banks fall and spring. Now, at eighty-four, she had flown over the river to ease the longing for the spruce forest that wrapped her in peace.

The river she loved sustained the rapids. The river she loved marked the seasons. Mountains of frozen froth built up in winter only to float away like a dream in spring. In summer, the banks were a shimmering silver and green of grass and forest. In the fall, hillsides along the flow were a bright yellow and soft brown, punctuated by the deep red of hibernating blueberry plants. The river she loved gave her food. Trout and pike swam in its depths. Beaver and muskrat lived along its banks. Moose foraged in its shallows. Black bears drank on its beaches. The river she loved was living, constantly changing shape and attitude. Spring flooding would tear down an island here, depositing silt somewhere else to build again. Banks crumbled and cherished trees were washed away. Familiar twists were reconstructed as the raging power of the spring flow cut across a meadow, changing the river's course. But always the huge rapids were there. Thundering. Cascading. Defying.

Because different people valued the rapids differently, courts were deciding their fate. Only the concerted effort of provincial utilities, international construction companies, and the most brilliant engineers in the world could destroy those rapids. Only the Crees, Annie's people, could save them. The producers and consumers of electricity fought for their demise. Hunters fought for their life. The Crees saw the river as a living thing. Entrepreneurs saw hundreds of millions of gallons of rushing water wasted daily. The fight was carried on, not near the rapids, not in the villages of the river's friends, but in the cities, where rivers and forests had long since been forced into productivity and were dead.

As a concession to the Crees, a wise arbitrator suggested that representatives of the river and of progress visit the people in their hunting camps to explain to them their choices. The river could remain the same or the river could be dammed. The dam would produce electricity that could be sold, bringing untold prosperity to the Crees of northern Quebec. My job was to accompany the people visiting the camps. I was seen as neutral.

The little fact-finding group had many camps to visit. Among them was the camp where Annie was staying. The research team was to visit camps and interview hunters in an attempt to discover concerns about the land and livelihood. James was the leader of the camp where Annie was staying. James's wife and parents were also at the camp. For some reason, none of Annie's grandchildren were there. Annie was the matriarch of the camp, even though she was a visitor.

Crees honour their elders by caring for them, listening to their advice, and learning from their stories. Annie was well cared for in the camp. She did her share of work as she could. Using a small cutting tool made of a razor blade and wood, she cut tanned moosehides into long, thin strips about one-quarter inch in width. Moosehide is thick. Annie was strong.

In a world where assembly lines build, pack, or sew almost everything, snowshoes were built by individuals. In a world where increased productivity is a goal and efficiency a measure, snowshoe building was family recreation on long winter nights. The whole family would gather to work on snowshoes, laughing and chatting in the oil lamplight. Small children would wrap moosehide string into a ball. The men would carve frames. Some women would string the snowshoes, while others would decorate the finished product.

Snowshoes last a few seasons of hard use. Everyone in a camp that could walk needed snowshoes. New pairs were always in demand. Several pairs were always at some stage of creation. Where a suburban family might play a board game, a Cree family, in the hunting camp, would work on snowshoes. Annie would sit on her knees in her corner cutting a moosehide into long thongs for weaving snowshoes. There were no young children to help, so when her pile of string was large enough by her estimation, she would wrap it into a ball.

The other women in the camp would string snowshoes while the men worked on a different set of frames each. The men sat on large sheets of plastic on the spruce bough floor to gather shavings, minimizing mess while collecting kindling for the fire. The shavings were placed in a bucket at the end of the work session and set near the stoves to dry.

Every job that could be done in the lodge was done together by the family. Rabbits were skinned on plastic in the lodge. Ducks, geese, and partridge were plucked. Moccasins were sewn. Mittens were made and clothes mended. It was all fun. It was all educational.

News of the day was shared. If someone did not have a task, he or she sat and listened, offering opinions where the opportunity presented itself. Anyone could chime in, young or old, and everyone usually did.

The elders told stories of the past, keeping deceased relatives alive in the corporate memory. They told of old traditions that were the foundation for modern Cree life. They explained past family and village decisions that had shaped local history. They passed down stories that gave the Crees their identity. With words, actions, tones, and expressions, the elders taught history and entertained.

By watching everyone work on snowshoe or mitt, night after night, the children learned the skills that their great-grandparents had taught their grandparents on long winter nights in the lodge.

Annie was honoured in the camp. She offered what she could towards the survival of the camp. Surrounded by a huge piece of plastic, she would begin the process of producing fur or food by skinning small animals. The bough floor masked the smell, while the plastic contained the mess of outdoor work brought indoors. Annie helped prepare meals by cutting meat for the pot. Her sharp knife and steady hand turned chunks of meat into uniformly thin steaks for the frying pan. Sometimes she mixed the dough for bannock, the camp's staple bread.

The single Otter we had chartered landed on the little frozen lake attempting to outrun a following cloud of propeller-driven snow. The entire camp turned out to meet us. This was an important time. The camp would hear the possibilities for their future and share their opinions. The government was actually sending people to listen to them.

A solemn reception line formed as the plane skied to a stop. After disembarking, each member of the party passed each person in the line. Right hands were firmly gripped with one shake up and one shake down. Not a word was spoken by anyone. This solemn formality, on a frozen lake, hundreds of miles from the village, struck me as funny. The line could have been a small graduation ceremony or part of a wedding—the reception line to nowhere. But mostly, I thought of a square dance. "Shake hands all—move down the line. Now, circle left. You're doin' fine. Follow your partner to the tent. Go inside with your back half bent." As each person finished the handshakes, they circled around the entire group walking up the path toward the lodge. The next person fell in behind, forming a line with an amazingly precise, random uniformity.

Several families living together in a 400-square-foot area need judicious rules of conduct. Each person, aware of all that takes place, lives as if nothing is seen or heard. Discipline is individual. Love is private. Disagreements are personal. Meals, prepared at the same time for convenience, are familial. Everyone eats in a restaurant atmosphere on a spruce bough floor, aware of the other families, but not interacting. When a camp has the chance to celebrate together, they become one family and enjoy each other.

Excited chattering began the instant the first person entered the lodge. Voices, excited to see a visitor, could be heard out to the lake. Pots of water were set to boil, chunks of bannock taken out of plastic bags. People seated themselves in their family areas waiting for the visit.

As I raised my head inside the tent flap, eyes slowly adjusting to the dim light, I saw Annie seated opposite the door. To my immediate right, a short distance from the lodge wall, was a red-and-white-checked dishtowel neatly spread on the spruce boughs. This was my seat. Looking around, I saw no other such accommodation for the other visitors. Maybe this was a statement. I sat down. Everyone sat somewhere near Annie, until she was engulfed in a circle of smiling, chattering faces. The men knelt, resting on their legs. The women sat on their legs, giving the impression of looking sideways. Both positions seemed uncomfortable to me. I adjusted myself every few moments, not used to sitting for great lengths of time without a chair. The two men who would explain the legal processes found seats near me. The pilot elected to stay near the plane. As the three of us were seated, the lodge went silent. One man, from a law firm, was carrying papers for signatures. One was a Cree who would translate and explain. Although I was to be the neutral witness to the process, I knew everyone in the tent was watching me as the token honest person for possible endorsement of the process.

A wonderful folding topographical map of the area appeared from a briefcase along with a collapsible stand. This impressed everyone. The map was well done, showing in vibrant colours the rivers, the areas to be flooded, and the size of the new lake to be formed by the dam. Detailed explanations were offered. A pointer showed the very place where we were seated to be only a short distance from the dammed water. Annie caught on very quickly.

She asked, with a daughter translating: "In the summer when water is low, the dam will hold back water for hydro. How will the fish live in a shallow river?"

The presenter was surprised that the old lady had jumped to the heart of the discussion. A swollen river presented logistical problems for travel and the loss of natural beauty such as the rapids. But a dry river meant a dramatic change in the environment. Annie had seen this. She was skeptical of any answer. She leaned back and lit her pipe, waiting.

Another folding chart was produced from the briefcase demonstrating that this question was foremost on everyone's mind. This chart was a beautiful cross-section of the river, showing the flow at both flood and dry times in comparison to the present level and the average level with the dams.

One hunter mentioned that the rise and fall of the water would make ice unstable and crossing difficult during the winter. Another asked if the salt water from the James Bay might not run in when the flow of water was light, ruining the water supply for the villages on the coast. All these questions were answered, some satisfactorily.

Then Annie spoke again. "There will be too much water sometimes. Fish will not spawn. Many trees will die."

A predetermined answer came quickly.

"It will take about three seasons for new spawning beds to develop. Trees, anywhere near the flooding, will be slashed long before the project is finished."

The question was answered without being understood. Annie smoked her pipe.

A group discussion among Crees is different. There is no competition, only informing. There is no interrupting. There is no feeling of superiority. Statements are often couched in lengthy stories or explanations filled with phrases translating to "further, I want to say" or "and again it will happen like this," joining sentences in a seamless monologue. The more important the statement, the longer the monologue. All listeners honour each speaker. Each speaker says everything to be said in one turn and ends with something like, "that is all I have to say." No questions are asked of speakers. Someone's statement may be affirmed by another speaker with a "John said . . . and this is good." No one criticizes or directly contradicts. Each one simply presents an idea to the others. The point is not to make the speaker look impressive, but to offer ideas to the discussion. Often someone briefly gives a summary when all have had their say.

After hearing many thoughts for and against the dam project, Annie assumed the role of moderator, summing up all that had been said.

"What we sign, we will be signing for everything that lives here with us. People far away will be able to read at night and stay warm when they don't have wood, if we sign. The water will rise and Mistassini Lake will get much bigger. Many trees will die and the fish will lose their homes for a while. Maybe our men will not be safe crossing small rivers and streams in the winter. Maybe the geese will not know where to land in the fall. The moose can move into the hills. If we sign and the water rises, then we won't have to go so far to carry water."

I marvelled at this summary. Annie had heard the questions, weighed the answers, and reduced the issue to its essence. She paused looking around the lodge, pipe in her teeth, smoke forming a soft haze where she sat. After a moment, she took the pipe from her mouth.

"Our names are important."

The Great Weasel Hunt

Jean Baptiste invited Billy and his family to hunt with him. In early September, they moved to his trapping ground, planning to stay until the spring thaw. The two families, ten people, with their winter supplies flew into the forest 250 miles from their home.

Billy was a happy, overweight man in his late fifties. The tiny broken blood vessels giving his nose and cheeks a bright red glow announced his hobby. In the village, he spent much of his time trying to escape the drudgery. In the hunting camp, others said, he was one of the best trappers around.

Jean Baptiste was tall and straight, keeping his grey/black hair short on the sides and standing on top. In his early sixties, he had the vigorous look of an outdoorsman. Jean Baptiste was always busy, but always happy to talk.

In their youth, Jean Baptiste and Billy would have made the arduous journey to their trapping grounds by canoe. But in these modern times, they had chartered a single Otter, a cigar with a propeller and wings, to carry them to their winter home. The Crees adapted easily to anything modern that enhanced their ability to hunt and fish. The chartered aircraft was such an adaptation. Although these men could still paddle for hours at a time, the bush plane turned ten days of hard paddling and portaging into a two-hour flight.

It was good for two or more families to hunt together. Work could be shared and long evenings made shorter. On the other hand, too many families sharing one camp could mean hardship when game was scarce. Jean Baptiste felt secure with Billy and his family.

Both families had moved into the temporary shelter of tents while building a log lodge before the winter snows came. Daily the two men had dropped tall, straight, black spruce trees with chain saws, another modern adaptation from the traditional axe they used so well. The women trimmed the branches from the trunks that would become the walls of the home shared for the entire winter by ten people. A month of concerted effort found everyone snug and content in a log lodge almost identical to those built by Jean Baptiste's great-grandfathers on the same trapping ground hundreds of years before the tallest tree that could be seen was even a seedling.

The Cree winter lodge is a marvel of adaptation in a beautiful but unforgiving environment. Jean Baptiste had built his winter dwelling in this tradition. The floor was dug into the ground to keep out winter winds. Logs were stacked about three feet higher than the dug-out area, forming a solid wall about six feet in height from floor to wall top. Logs, skinned of bark inside to reflect the light of candles or oil lamps, were chinked with moss to seal cracks. Split-log planks, converging from walls to a small opening in the centre of the lodge, formed the roof. The overlapped roofing planks had a slight pitch to encourage water to run off and snow to build an insulating depth. A thick layer of sphagnum moss was added over the planks to seal out the weather. The moss was not waterproof, but absorbent, holding rain or thawing snow until it dried in wind and sun. Sphagnum moss was an ancient diaper.

Firewood was piled two rows deep and six feet high on either side of the lodge entrance, offering easy access to fuel and protection from wind. A panel of tent canvas formed the door, held down by a heavy stick fit into two cloth holders sewn on each side of the flap. The smooth stick weighed down the flap, forming a handle to pull from the outside and push on from the inside. Once released, the flap automatically fell into place.

The lodge was spacious, although dark. Two tin wood-burning stoves, one for each family, filled the centre of the room. Two tin chimneys extended through the hole in the ceiling. Around the edge of the lodge were neatly rolled blankets. Shelves at the top of the log wall held clothes and personal things. Food was stored near the door, with each family having a side for their larder. Smaller outbuildings, completely snow covered, held other necessities of life that could not fit into the lodge.

The most unique feature of the lodge was the spruce-bough floor. The lodge site was chosen by the women in the family to be near water and a good source of spruce boughs. The young women were responsible for laying down the floor. They broke short pieces of the flat, fanned bough from the small spruce trees and wove them into a fragrant blanket onto the dirt floor of the lodge. Snow on moccasins melted through the boughs. Liquid spilled quickly disappeared through them. The inside of the lodge always smelled clean and fresh. Everyone walked, sat or slept on a soft, but firm, surface. The boughs were replaced weekly, and laid in such a way as to not lift when things were dragged over them. Laying a spruce bough floor was an art; a skill learned through observation and practice.

The Cree winter lodge, *"Tagachtaogomoak"* or "the place of being," was weathertight. The occupants' breath was warm enough to keep water from freezing at night. During the day, each family had a stove burning. The heat could be extreme, forcing occupants to lie on the floor for comfort.

I was visiting the Baptiste camp, as I did many hunting camps, bringing gifts and news of the village as well as dreaded schoolwork and some inspiration for those who were away from home for months at a time. The Hudson's Bay Store manager also visited the camps, bringing much-needed supplies and buying furs, the result of a winter's work.

The manager was to visit the Baptiste camp in a few days. Shopping lists were discussed, furs prepared, and a lunch menu planned. There would be a planeload of goods, from lard to shotgun shells. If the camp didn't get what they needed on this visit, they would have to go without for the winter. The manager would price the furs harvested. A winter hunt was pure speculation. The Hudson's Bay Store extended credit based on the hunter's ability. The manager's visit midway through the winter represented the first installment on that credit.

Everyone but the youngest grandchildren was lying on the spruce-bough floor speculating about the current price of chain saw oil and whether or not the manager would remember hotdogs, when Smally ran into the lodge. Smally, a diminutive six-year-old who looked like he wore an inner tube under his parka, screamed that there was a weasel on top of the woodpile.

My Cree was passable, but the excitement in Smally's voice hid the meaning of his words, at least from me. Obviously everyone else understood, leaping up as if the spruce floor were on fire. I knew at once that no one was stealing the woodpile, but I was not at all sure of why six relaxing adults would rush outside, into snow and frigid air, without coats or moccasins, just to see a weasel.

Often, after hunting, Cree men take off their moccasins, airing out the duffle liners and socks that kept their feet warm in the moosehide-covered ball. Damp feet were uncomfortable at best, and at worst would freeze quickly. Gumboots rolled down to the ankle were worn like slippers when someone went outside after removing his or her moccasins. In the camp's excitement, even gumboots were forgotten.

Billy, who spoke only enough English to find a bathroom at a gas station, ran through the flap, yelling, "Weasel, weasel!" As I passed through the flap, I wondered how much damage a weasel could do in a camp like this. The potential for destruction, it seemed to me, must be extensive to generate this kind of excitement.

Once I was outside, it became apparent that the weasel had disappeared into the woodpile. I had seen Jean Baptiste and Billy silently stalk to within twenty yards of a moose in a clearing. I had helped these men meticulously set beaver traps, disturbing as little of the surrounding area as possible. I had heard them talk to geese, calling motionless in a willow blind. Here, in front of me, was the entire camp running and jumping and shouting like children with a broken piñata—except for Smally. He stood intently peering here and there into the woodpile, wearing alternatively a triumphant smile and a determined scowl. I could mark the movements of the weasel by Smally's quiet slide from place to place in front of the pile of wood.

"It's right here!" he stated in an extremely loud whisper.

Suddenly the camp was galvanized into action, with Jean Baptiste and Billy choreographing the scene. Billy wisely instructed all the women and children to surround the woodpile, making sure that the weasel did not leave the general vicinity. This produced mixed reactions. The children were jubilant with the prospect of chasing a weasel. Two of the women, thinking beyond the moment, wondered what would happen if the weasel came at them. This gave Billy pause, but he seemed to sense that the women could intimidate the weasel sufficiently to keep it from escaping. I couldn't help wondering if he had learned from experience.

Jean Baptiste took a more direct approach to the situation. Going directly to where Smally was peering into the woodpile, he began removing wood, piece by piece. This only served to heighten the excitement. The women realized that this could chase the weasel towards them. Smally realized that he might get the weasel. The other children realized that the weasel might soon pop out at one of the women. Being practical, I wondered who would rebuild the woodpile.

To my surprise, Jean Baptiste picked up a long, slender piece of wood and brought it to me. "*Oota!* Here!" he said, holding out the piece of wood. "*Otomoha ai paicheeitotaite!* Hit him when he comes." He wanted me to dispatch the weasel. I couldn't believe it. Maybe he thought, "The Minister hits people over the head with his sermons—why not a weasel with a chunk of wood."

I was determined not to let him down.

Smally's twelve-year-old sister was called *Tanis*, "daughter" in Cree. I never knew her given name. I don't think she did either. She offered some advice in English. "Don't squish it."

I realized that Billy and Jean Baptiste were not protecting the camp, but attempting to provide Smally with his first pelt to present to the Hudson's Bay manager.

There are orchestrated, formal rites of passage for children in all cultures, like the Walking Out Ceremony, bar mitzva, baptism, or vision quest. But the milestones of growth, the first step, the first word, the first day of school, the first bundle of spruce boughs, or the first pelt, are parental gauges of growth toward who a child should be. Jean Baptiste had recognized such a milestone, and was determined to make it happen. Apparently, killing and skinning the animal was not as important as the act of presenting the little pelt to the trader. The success of this particular milestone depended upon my ability to dispatch the weasel with a chunk of wood.

Smally stood next to the woodpile, marking the weasel's hiding place. Billy and Jean Baptiste gingerly removed piece after piece of wood.

"Pekach. Slowly," Billy breathed, not wanting to disturb the little animal.

I don't know anything about the emotional state of weasels, but I was sure this one was either hysterical with fright or laughter, given the scene around the woodpile. The women were still at their posts yelling instructions and holding coats tightly against a leap from the woodpile. The young people were still stationed, calling insults to Smally and teasing the women by saying they saw the weasel about to jump in someone's direction. Jean Baptiste and Billy were dismantling the woodpile in slow motion. I was hovering here and there, brandishing the log.

Gradually excitement heightened. Smally had not seen the weasel move. The woodpile was shrinking to where it was hiding.

"Egwani," Jean Baptiste said in a low growl. "Enough."

Was he going to spare the weasel? After all, suffering thirty minutes of terror was as good as being a pelt. Had he decided that the weasel was not a worthy pelt? My thoughts were interrupted as he stood before me, hand held out. He wanted my log.

Somehow, while dismantling the woodpile and issuing a myriad of instructions to all participants, Jean Baptiste had come to the realization that I should not be the difference between a pelt to present to the trader and escape. I was not sure that setting beaver traps or shooting big game adequately qualified someone to be a weasel basher, or that preaching and visiting camps disqualified others; but Jean Baptiste had made up his mind. Reluctantly, I relinquished my log and became an observer in this familial adventure. I was relieved to see that Jean Baptiste himself was going to wield the log. It would have been humiliating to have one of the children take over that responsibility.

Billy now had sole responsibility for dismantling the woodpile. As he lifted a particularly strategic log, Smally saw the weasel again.

He pointed and yelled, "*Oota. Oota!*"

The weasel saw its chance and leapt. It leapt right at Billy, hitting him in the chest, and clinging to his partially zipped parka. I suppose that once the weasel realized he had chosen a tree that jumped around, he decided to hide in the darkest place possible, so he pulled himself inside Billy's parka. Jean Baptiste proved his worth as a hunter. He cautiously moved next to Billy, log held high. This was not an easy feat, as Billy was jumping and yelling and waving his arms. Without warning, during one of Billy's downward arm flings, Jean Baptist delivered a crushing blow, with the log, to Billy's chest at the spot where he calculated the weasel to be hiding. Billy stood stunned for a brief moment and then clutched his chest, staggered back a few steps and finally, after swaying in place for a few seconds, fell forward. As he hit the ground, knees first, closely followed by his upper body, the weasel popped out the lower back of his parka and disappeared into the snow and trees.

The tension broke. Everyone but Billy dissolved into spasms of laughter. Billy rolled onto his back smiling and holding his chest. Smally attempted to follow tiny tracks to a new hiding place. The women were laughing and wiping tears from their eyes. The children were gloating over the fact that Smally now had no pelt.

Eventually, Jean Baptiste stopped laughing.

"Too bad Billy didn't fall on his back."

Tents and Trees

The Crees claim they took their land of forest, lakes, and rivers from the Iroquois because of a wealth of furs and wild game. The Iroquois counter with tales of driving the Crees north away from the desirable land of moderate climate in southern Ontario and Quebec. In any case, I was living in a tiny Cree village on a huge, beautiful inland lake, sixty miles of gravel road away from the closest town. I wanted to make for myself a weekend getaway camp to enjoy the beautiful countryside.

The village sat on the southern end of a narrow flow of water linking two lakes and forming a body of water covering almost 4,000 square miles. The lake was isolated and beautiful. Long, lonely beaches of white sand spotted the winding shoreline. Tall fingers of sand deposited by glaciers eons ago stretched out here and there, forming bays sheltered from wind and wave. Hills of black spruce and poplar rose from the water's edge, home to animals great and small, fierce and timid, predator and prey. Rivers and streams poured into the lake or formed at the lake flowing hundreds of miles away. The beauty was overwhelming, as was the village busyness.

The road from town to village was beautiful regardless of the season. Spring brought the smell of wild flowers sprinkling colour through the grassy meadows and the song of thaw-swollen streams cascading to the big lake. Fall painted a blaze of yellow-turning poplars and blue carpets of lowbush blueberries. Summer carried the sultry smell of shoreline and spruce trees. Winter built a thick, insulating blanket of snow on the land, providing surrealistic ice sculptures where the road traversed frozen rapids.

I had admired, for some time, a particularly beautiful spot on the road that happened to be at the only intersection for about 120 miles. Sixty miles from town, one made a left turn to drive another fifteen miles to the village. At that intersection was a beautiful river with an enthusiastic set of rapids falling to a broad pool after passing under the road before flowing gently on. The rapids formed a turning staircase, with each drop flowing for some twenty-five yards before dropping once again toward the pool. These surging plateaus were as uniform as a landscaper's garden. Each plateau was bordered by a small glen of spruce trees reminiscent of a James Fenimore Cooper novel. After several exploratory hikes upstream along the rapids, I found a glen in which to build my retreat.

The site was perfect. It was far enough up the river to provide solitude, yet close to the road for easy accessibility, even on snowshoes. There was a small clearing for a tent sheltered by mature spruce trees. Just below the rapids at the beginning of my glen's plateau was a large, flat rock from which water could be bucketed with ease without intrusion of sand or sticks.

A site chosen, I set out to get the things I needed for my retreat. I asked MaryAnn if she would make me a tent. Most of the women in the village could quickly sew a canvas wall tent of any dimension. The canvas panels were three feet wide, so the walls became multiples of three appropriate for the size of a family. My tent was to be nine feet by twelve. These tents were a marvel, easy to pitch, weathertight and comfortable.

Usually a ridgepole traversed the length of the tent held up, front and rear, by the apex of crossed poles. The ridge did not sit above the tent tied with canvas strips. It didn't simply enter the tent through crude holes. The ridgepole was inserted into the tent through foot-long sleeves that helped keep summer bugs at bay. The walls were variable in length, designed to be tied to a spruce frame positioned far enough from the tent to allow for maximum width. Strings attached to the seam between roof and wall panel were tied to the frame, creating strength and width. Excess canvas at the bottom of the walls was folded away from the tent. A log the length of the particular wall was placed on this extra material, making that wall almost bug-proof, and secure from winds and rain.

MaryAnn and her husband were good friends of mine. By asking her to make the tent, I hoped to solve two problems at once. I would get a beautifully made tent and, hopefully, help from Matthew, MaryAnn's husband, with setting up my camp.

I had other things to pick up as well as the tent. A small tin wood stove would heat my tent. All Cree tents, except summer travelling tents, had stoves to one side of the entrance. The stoves usually sat on four wooden pegs driven into the ground. The stovepipe protruded either out the front panel and up, or straight up through the roof. I preferred the pipe out the front of the tent so that rain or melting snow did not drip down onto my stove.

I needed plywood and wooden stakes to build shelves for cooking implements, utensils, cutlery, and dishes. Things like salt and pepper shakers, string, buckets for water, canisters for sugar, flour and the like, flashlights, candles, matches, and many other small items, needed to be gathered. I had a good idea of what I needed for comfort and practicability, having camped in one form or another all my life.

Unfortunately, my need to get away was occurring in the dead of winter. My little streamside glen was covered with eight feet of snow! The staircase of rapids had spots of moving water fast enough to resist the grip of cold, but the stream was like shredded glass. I had never attempted winter camping, but was inspired to try by the Crees. The Crees hunted in the winter, setting up camp when they were further than a day's walk from the main lodge. I had stayed in the warm log lodges where the breath of fifteen or so people kept water from freezing at night. I had also awakened in hastily pitched tents with two inches of breath frost on my sleeping bag. Winter camping seemed clean and bug-free. I knew I would need help to be successful in my winter endeavour.

As I hoped, Matthew volunteered to help me set up camp. We loaded tent and trappings into my truck and set out for the frozen river by the road. We had axe and chainsaw, sledgehammer and nails—tools for finish carpentry in the bush. Most important, we had snowshoes and snow shovels.

Matthew was a veteran "bush-man," successfully bridging the gap between modern administrator and traditional hunter. Friend and expert, Matthew was the perfect person to help with the camp. He was energetic, enthusiastic and skilled. We began by clearing the site I had chosen. I soon realized that Matthew had no intention of pitching a tent on the first day we worked together. He approved of the spot by the creek, but indicated that the tent would be incorrectly placed facing the creek.

I wanted to see the frozen river and escaping rapids as I stepped out of the tent in the morning. Matthew indicated that the tent should face the road, actually, not the road, but the rising sun. This made no sense to me. For one thing, I wanted a little privacy. For another, with short winter days, the sun would not be up when I left the tent in the morning. In the summer, the trees blocked the sun, for the most part.

When I mentioned these concerns, Matthew replied, "Tents face the sun."

We set about clearing the site. Had it been summer, all sticks and branches from the surrounding trees would have been picked up. Small stumps and rocks would have been located and eliminated. The entire area would have been raked free of forest debris. Because this site was sloped, dirt would have been removed at the back to level an area for the tent.

But it was winter. In his snowshoes, Matthew paced off an area quite a bit bigger than the tent and began shovelling out the snow. I had done a lot of snow shovelling as a boy, earning money by cleaning driveways. This was different. There were no snow shovels, but two huge spoons carved of wood about four feet in length with canoe paddle handles sprouting long, oval-shaped concave scoops. Like paddles, they were light but very strong. A kind of backhand motion, pulling the scoop across the body, top hand facing away and bottom hand turned toward the body, enabled one to throw snow quite a long way to the rear.

Shovelling snow at a house in the suburbs is controlled, because the snow must be stacked and stored. We began throwing snow anywhere outside the snowshoe square. I asked the first of many apparently silly questions.

"Shouldn't we throw the snow further? It will be too deep outside the tent to get in." This seemed obvious. The three feet of snow removed from the tent space made the depth just outside that space an extra three feet.

"No," Matthew replied from just outside a cloud of snow flying beyond the boundaries of my tent space.

The inflection in that one word was amazing. There was no impatience or anger. There was no surprise or condescension. That one word said, "We are doing this just the way it should be done. There is quite a bit of snow in this square so we need to keep working."

Matthew was a few years younger than I but a little taller. He was lean, with the weathered good looks of an outdoorsman. Matthew was part of a generation of Crees that straddled two cultures. He was an expert hunter, following the lead of his father and grandfather; but he had a college degree and was now working on a master's degree, planning to guide his people along the narrow path of stability into the modern world. Matthew was soft-spoken and not given to small talk. He was direct and honest, ignoring many of the cultural niceties of modern society used to temper opinions and ingratiate listeners. When Matthew asked, "How are you?" He really wanted to know. His wiry strength was augmented by the ability to pace his work, finding a rhythm when walking, cutting wood, or shovelling snow, that allowed him to work for long periods of time without resting. Not talking was part of his work rhythm.

"Okay. I guess we can make a path to the door when the tent is up," I observed, not being one to let go of a concept easily.

"Wait first, Jim."

This was a curious expression of unclear meaning. Should the question be asked again in a little while? Or would it be answered in a few moments after some thought? I decided that the response meant, "Let's finish clearing the snow as I suggested it be done, and then we can talk about the things that you would like to do."

My parents used to give answers like that. "We'll see." Later, when I would complain: "But you said . . ." they would say, "No, I didn't." And they were right.

We removed about three of the six or seven feet of snow from the tent area. Matthew worked steadily, saying very little.

"Get the snowshoes. Now we pack the snow," Matthew instructed.

We had used snowshoes for the short walk from the road to the site. We took them off and waded into the snow to shovel. I watched Matthew, snowshoes on once again, stomp the perimeter of the cleared snow square in ever-decreasing, concentric squares, packing the snow two inches or so at each step.

Cree snowshoes were a marvel of bush technology; handmade art with several styles for different jobs. We were using long shoes with frames rounded up at the front and tapered at the rear. They were for walking quickly in the bush, designed to slip through forks in trees and bushes. The frames were hand-carved of birch to an almost completely square three-quarters of an inch per side, bent by steaming the wood at the toe, and joined in a tail at the rear. The web was closely woven moosehide painstakingly cut with a razor to twine-thickness strings, handwoven in a close pattern for the light, fluffy snow conditions of the frigid winters in northern Quebec.

Were we to tamp snow in a less cold climate with these snowshoes, the weight of snow would make it very difficult. This powdery snow just shook off each time we lifted a foot. The Crees had designed a perfect snowshoe for this kind of work in this kind of climate.

"I don't mind shovelling it all. It would be nice to be on bare ground."

"You need some snow. Just walk on it now." Matthew was stomping while talking, packing the snow bit by bit in the cleared square.

I put on my snowshoes. Two thin rawhide straps made it easy to slip my foot into the strap perpendicular to the snowshoe. Standing on the back of the snowshoe with the other foot, the foot in the strap was pointed toe down with the heel lifted and turned until the toe was under the cross harness. No hands were needed. The tension on the two straps at the back of the heel held the foot in place. The process was reversed to step out of the snowshoe.

After being stomped for about ten minutes, the snow had compacted about another six inches. Matthew looked around and smiled. His face lit with the smile of straight white teeth and flashing dark eyes.

"It won't snow tonight," he predicted. "Tomorrow we'll come back in the morning. The trail and clearing will be frozen. It will be easy to work. I have to get back now."

We put the few tools we had in the back of the truck and drove back to the village. Matthew climbed out of the truck. "Just leave everything in the back. We'll need it tomorrow. Nine o'clock. Okay?"

"Okay, see you then. Thanks, Matthew. I am really going to enjoy this tent."

My first thought as I turned the truck around was to finish the camp. How hard could it be? Mind made up, I went back to the tent site eager to complete my retreat. Matthew had shown me the kind of poles to cut for the tent frame, but I had a better idea. If I turned the tent the way I wanted to in the first place, so it faced the river, I could take advantage of two nice, straight spruce trees as poles, eliminating the need to cut four poles to support the front and the back.

I did cut a ridgepole that was dry with no bark long enough to span my two spruce trees. Without much effort, I slipped the ridgepole into one sleeve, through the tent, and out the other sleeve. Once through the tent, the ridgepole had only to be lashed to the two spruce trees. I lifted one end of the pole up to what seemed a reasonable height for the walls, and lashed it to the tree. Stepping back, I had to admit that the tent looked a little like a sheet hung out to dry there between the two trees. I felt pride in pitching the tent by myself.

The tent was almost up. There were still walls to square, stove and pipe to assemble, and the spruce bough floor to gather and weave. Four strings were attached to each side of the tent, one at each corner, and two on the back designed to tie to a frame, holding the walls of the tent out. Building a frame seemed a great deal of work. Tying the strings to sharpened poles driven into the ground seemed more efficient to me. Once the poles were secured, I tied strings to sticks pulling the wall out and up, squaring the tent. The hanging sheet was transformed into a tent.

MaryAnn had known I wanted a stove in the tent. She assumed the pipe would exit through the front panel. She had cut a hole leaving the canvas flaps to dangle across the opening. I did not understand why she had left the flaps until I found the piece of tin Matthew had given me. The tin was about a foot square. Matthew had cut a small hole in the centre and then cut back diagonally toward each corner from that centre hole. It was obvious that these tins flaps were to be bent back. I placed the tin up to the hole in the wall and pushed one flap back. It opened the hole. This procedure was done with each tin flap. Curious, I went outside to see what a stove flange in a tent looked like. It looked awful outside. The tin flaps stuck out straight with the entire piece threatening to fall inside. I bent the flaps back flat against the tent by putting my fingers in the hole and pulling and pushing the flap. The bits of tent that had covered the opening became material to which a tin flap could adhere. That being completed, I set the stove itself on a cement block and began to assemble about six two-foot pieces of three-inch tin stovepipe.

Stovepipe is flat for shipping and storage prior to sale. One side, along the length, has a groove that fits the other side with a ridge. In theory, placing the ridge and groove together will allow the natural springiness of the tin to lock the piece into its useful cylindrical form—in theory. After about four attempts apiece, all pipe was together and all digits were intact.

Building the cylinders was easy compared to fitting them together. First the decision had to be made as to whether the piece above fit into the piece below or vice-versa. It seemed to me that the downward piece should be a "guzinta," so that drippings from wood or moisture would not stain the pipe. On the other hand, it was definitely easier to slip a piece down and over than down and in.

All tin stovepipe has a flared end and a fluted end. The fluted end goes in. Again, theory states that the flutes allow the pipe to easily fit into the flare. One must press against the flutes with fingers near the top, while pushing the pipe into the flared end of another piece. If the piece fits over too easily, fingers get cut. If it won't go inside and the whole thing slips, fingers get cut. Facial expressions and language are crucial tools for stovepipe assembly. I could tell early on that I would need both.

After about forty-five minutes, my stovepipe was near completion. I had a forty-five-degree piece, pre-assembled, going out the wall. The only challenge remaining was fitting the pipe into the stove. With a fit that seemed impossibly tight, and my hands growing cold, I decided to augment the fluting by cutting some of my own with a pair of pliers. The idea worked. Pipe and stove were one.

Although there was much work left to complete the retreat, I decided to wait until Matthew arrived at 9:00 the next morning to help. I was not sure how to weave a spruce bough floor. I was not completely clear on the idea of building shelving out of sticks and plywood. Most importantly, I was not sure I wanted to build a fire in the stove on my own and take a chance on burning down the tent. Although the tent was pitched in a non-traditional way, I knew that Matthew would be pleased that this piece of work was completed.

The next morning was clear and cold. Breath froze on cheeks. Matthew and I arrived at my campsite. He was right. The trail to the camp and all snowshoe-packed ground was frozen solid. We could walk anywhere without sinking to our waists in snow.

At the end of the trail Matthew stopped. "You shouldn't hang your tent in the trees."

I supposed this to be enough criticism for Matthew to offer in one day, because he was gracious enough not to mention that the tent was facing the wrong direction. I thought it looked pretty good.

"It was faster to do it this way." I regretted offering this little thought as soon as it was said.

To my surprise, Matthew forged ahead with the camp. "I will check your stove, and then we fix the walls and the floor."

Our work began. The day was different. We chatted as we worked. We talked of fishing, hunting, friends, the city, Cree politics, and the church. Matthew had thrown large rectangles of cardboard in the back of the truck. Now we used them. He cut hefty logs and laid them along the excess tent on each wall. This held the tent down. Then we piled snow up the wall.

"The snow close to the tent will melt and freeze and keep out the draft."

Of course, ice near one's back would be cold; so the cardboard formed a rough wainscoting around the interior of the tent, keeping the cold from radiating through.

The most interesting part of fixing the camp was finding and preparing the spruce bough floor. Spruce boughs were used because they were soft, smelled wonderful, and absorbed spills.

Matthew simply taught. "The women choose a campsite for good water and boughs. The men hunt where the women say because the lodge needs to be good. There are no good boughs around here."

I looked around and saw nothing but spruce boughs everywhere. "Next time you will look for boughs."

"Well, there is plenty of water," I pointed out somewhat defensively.

One Man's MILE

"Yes," Matthew conceded. "And it is moving. That is very good."

Matthew began a short course in picking spruce boughs. We put our snowshoes on and went over to a stand of relatively small spruce trees, about twenty-five feet in height.

"These are too big," Matthew informed me. "The boughs are too spread." Pointing to a small spruce off to the side, "This is good," he instructed. "When you break off the end, it will grow back with another good bough next year. The tree gets thicker with more good boughs but they don't spread out like the big trees."

I thought to myself, *The Crees know the secret to Christmas tree pruning.*

The instruction continued. "You break it at this part of the branch and break up like this."

Matthew broke off a bough about ten inches from the end at a main stem holding a symmetrical pattern of six offshoots. "It doesn't matter how big, they just need to be thick." He snapped the branch up and it broke cleanly. "It breaks now in the cold, but if you break up, it will always break fast. See here: I broke this branch up. Here is an old break. The bear did this to chew on. He always breaks down."

After breaking what seemed to be a huge pile of boughs that were obviously not to Matthew's liking, we carried them to the tent. On the way, Matthew set his pile down near a scrawny alder sticking up through the snow. "Moose ate here—see, it is not brown, so it was this winter, but there are no tracks, so it was long ago." He pointed out a broken branch on the little bush. When I looked closely, I could see that some branches were broken near the ends and others at the main branch farther up.

"This is the cow," Matthew informed me, pointing to the small break. "She is dainty and takes small bites. This is the bull. He takes big bites. Unless he is scared, the moose always stops to eat, so you can tell what you are following this way. If there are no good tracks, you will know who is around."

Picking up his pile of boughs, Matthew walked along the narrow snowshoe trail back to the tent clearing. Stacking our boughs in the centre of the tent, we began to make a floor.

"My mother would not have allowed my father to do this. It is the woman's job, but MaryAnn and I do it together."

Matthew showed me how to lay the boughs down, beginning in the far corner of the tent. The natural bend in the bough was laid down and the next one was pushed inside the first about halfway under. The third was pushed into the other two, but about halfway on top, and so on. It took a while, but eventually the entire floor of the tent was covered with thick boughs. It was obvious that the floor was both comfortable and practical. Soft for sitting and lying down, sweet-smelling, and porous for spills, the floor was ingenious. Over the winter, boughs replaced weekly would form a wonderfully thick carpet that was biodegradable.

"It's time for tea," Matthew observed.

Matthew brought his backpack from the truck and placed it in a corner of the tent. I got the wood that was thrown in the truck bed and stacked it behind the stove. Matthew went to the nearby trees and gathered the grey moss that hung in the spruce branches.

"Old man's beard—good fire starter," he observed.

He then took the axe and shaved a pile of slivers from a piece of dry wood brought from the village. Placing the old man's beard in the bottom of the stove with the shavings on top, Matthew lit a match and pushed it through the circular draft in the front bottom centre of the tin stove. Draft sucked the small flame through the tinder up to the stovepipe. The fire blazed. Matthew dropped in a few small pieces of wood. Within five minutes, the tent was warm. After ten minutes the stove was glowing a pale red and the tent was getting too hot.

I went to get water for the tea while Matthew worked on a shelf. Once at the first accessible plateau in the icy stream, I dipped a five-gallon lard pail into the small cascade at the edge of a snow-covered flat rock and scooped a bucket of clean, fresh water. Back in the tent, Matthew set the water on the stove in a saucepan and proceeded to place a rectangular one-by-four piece of plywood on four stakes he had managed to drive into the frozen ground. This made a little shelf, actually two little shelves, for pots and pans, sugar, tea, etc.

As we drank our tea, Matthew commented, "It's good and warm in here. Make lots of wood for outside. I could help you make poles to hold the ridgepole."

"The trees work pretty well. It was easier this way." I missed the message in Matthew's words.

"When the trees move in the wind so will the tent," Matthew observed.

"That's okay—I won't be here for that long at a time," I commented, still missing the point.

"People will think your tent looks funny." Now Matthew was getting more direct.

"That's okay—if they don't like it they don't have to look at it," I said, laughing—still not getting the hint.

"Okay. Are you staying here tonight?"

"No, I have to get my sleeping bag and things. Is it okay to leave everything in the tent once I bring it out here?" I asked, thinking it would be nice not to have to prepare for every visit.

"Sure, no one will take anything. We leave everything. If someone is cold and sees the tent they might use your wood, but they would give it back." Matthew was unequivocal. His tone indicated that he was a bit insulted on behalf of the entire village. Trust and honesty were tent poles of the Cree society.

"I should get back," Matthew said. "Let me know when you will be out. I will have tea."

The Crees loved to visit, but often there was a pretext upon which the visit was based. Matthew wanted to check on me. I think it would be bad luck to have the minister, in your village, to die while camping.

We talked about hunting and hockey during the drive to the village. The tent was used weekly until March, when things got very busy at the church. It offered quiet days to snowshoe in the forest, and still nights for reading and deep sleep. In the early spring, my visits were short, just long enough to shake fallen snow off the tent. Matthew did visit often. There is not too much better than sharing a cup of tea with a friend, talking about everything while lying on a spruce bough floor with your head propped on a sleeping bag.

In mid-April, Matthew came by the house. "We should take the tent down now."

"Really? I thought I would use it all summer if I can stand the bugs," I replied. I knew there were trout in the little cascades and pickerel in the pool at the bottom. I was looking forward to warm summer nights in the tent.

"We should take it down. You can put it back up if you want to," Matthew suggested in an uncharacteristically illogical line of thought.

"No, I think I will leave it up."

Matthew never got impatient. He simply changed directions. "It's a nice day, if we ride on the side of the road we can take my skidoo."

The spring thaw had come, making travel in the bush hazardous because of soft snow and stumps and sticks. The north side of the road still had high snowbanks that protected a thin layer of ice/snow on the road itself from the sun. Snow machines would travel on that narrow road for another month.

"Okay, sounds fun. I haven't been out there for two weeks, so I should check on it anyway."

We took off down the road with a roar. The spring sun reflecting off the snow tanned face and hands quickly. We stopped on the road and walked up my well-used trail. The thaw had weakened the snow, and often one foot would punch through up to the hip. Going was slow and we laughed a lot.

"Think light," Matthew laughed. "That is what the Crees do in the spring."

We got to the tent with lighthearted effort. There it hung, suspended on the ridgepole, two feet in the air, like a blanket drying in the wind. Although it looked like the trees had grown, in fact the snow had melted from under the tent. Suddenly Matthew's hints came back to me.

He began to laugh, summing up all his ignored advice: "Sometimes tents and trees don't mix."

The Water Hole

The DeHavilland Beaver is an old, single-engine plane. Versatile enough to land on wheels, floats, or skis, it is the workhorse of the north. On this particular day, the Beaver landed on skis in a short-lived, propeller-generated blizzard across a frozen lake in northern Quebec. From the air, the lake resembled a bowl full of milk. No trees ran down to the shoreline of this little lake. Rather, grey granite boulders ringed the lake, keeping the frozen water inside, breaking only to accommodate a path to the hunting camp I was visiting.

I visited Cree hunting camps in the winter, flying up to 300 miles from the village of Mistassini Lake in Quebec. The Crees went into the bush in the fall, pursuing their traditional life of hunting and trapping. They returned to the village in the late spring. I visited the camps as any pastor visits any parishioners.

These camps were small, self-sufficient family enclaves dispersed throughout thousands of square miles of northern Quebec forest. Each camp was located in a carefully chosen area of a trapping ground. The trapping ground had been handed down from father to son for centuries. Care of the land was a sacred trust, so camps were moved from year to year to allow the land in one area to recover after a season of trapping. A camp usually consisted of a large, spruce-log lodge with a split log and canvas roof and a small outbuilding for storing the necessities of life. The lodges were built in the early fall for warmth and comfort. Up to four families, parents and children, coexisted all winter in these lodges without serious altercations. The Crees had a tacit understanding of communal living that rivalled any social structure in the world. They judiciously avoided being judgmental or interfering.

This was Isaiah's camp. Isaiah was a sixty-year-old trapper with a classically native face browned by long days of sun reflected off snow. His two sons and their infinite supply of children were hunting with him and Anna, his wife. Isaiah was always laughing boisterously at the children, chuckling at the events of life. The whole camp turned out to greet me. Children were jumping off the boulder ring and rolling in the snow. Dogs barked from their tethers somewhere back near the camp. The three older women huddled together where the path met the lake.

The three men came out to the plane. Isaiah stepped forward, extending his hand.

"*Wachiya!*" he shouted over the idling engine. Although rarely speaking English, he understood a great deal. He enjoyed practising his English with me, because he knew if he got stuck over a word I would practise my Cree to help him out.

"Good see you! Cold here!"

"Good to see you, too, Isaiah," I affirmed, grasping his hand.

His hands were warm. The traditional moosehide mitten that kept his hand warm hung from its string at his side. In turn, I shook each hand in the greeting party and lifted each child as he or she screamed with laughter.

"Have tea," Isaiah suggested.

I knew enough about Cree culture to know that this was an unusual request. In my culture, having coffee or tea was a catalyst for conversation. A hostess might ask, "Can I bring you some tea?" or "I have coffee on, would you like some?" Serving, holding, and sipping were "lull-in-the-conversation-filling" actions. But a Cree hostess would offer tea at the *end* of a visit. After the tea was finished, it was time to go. The hostess controlled the length of the visit. Tea signalled the end.

I was sure that Isaiah was being considerate because I had just arrived. He could probably see that I was half frozen from the one-and-one-half-hour plane ride in minus thirty-degree skies. I followed him across the frozen lake, through the break in the boulders, up the path to his camp.

Like most hunters expecting winter visitors by plane, Isaiah had marked a landing strip with small spruce trees. Six- or seven-foot trees were placed in two long rows out across the lake about ten feet apart. The green boughs, visible from a great distance against the snow, marked a landing strip in the midst of a sea of white. This was important for bush pilots flying in the winter, because they knew that there would be no serious snowdrifts or ice crevices between that line of trees. They knew the strip had been checked and they could land safely. We walked a short distance down this spruce corridor before crossing the boulder boundary.

Walking up the frozen path cut three feet deep in the snow, I could see what looked like a huge snowdrift, but people were moving into its centre. Everyone was moving into this circular, white snow mound. Only a glimpse of log exposed here and there by the warmth of the sun revealed that the mound was a winter lodge.

Getting closer, I could see a thin line of white smoke emerging from the top of the snow mound. From further down the path, it had been diffused by the tall spruces near the lodge. Although four stovepipes poked through the snow like errant twigs, there was only one fire. The straight line of smoke demonstrated a total lack of wind outside while promising warmth inside.

There are much better ways to judge cold than thermometers. When the inside of your nose freezes quickly in the open air, it's cold. When your breath freezes on your collar, you can be sure it's very cold. When there are millions of moisture crystals frozen in the air shining like diamonds in the sun, it is extremely cold. I noticed that my nose had frozen. As well, my collar was white from just the few moments of walking through the shimmering moisture frozen in the air on the way from plane to lodge.

Ducking down to move through the firewood windbreak stacked on either side of the canvas door flap, we entered the tent to sauna-like warmth and the permeating smell of spruce.

People were seated around the floor, which was a carpet of spruce boughs woven tightly together. The inside was dark enough to force eyes to adjust, even though sunlight from the stovepipe opening reflected off skinned spruce log walls.

Isaiah asked for tea. Mary, his wife, did a kind of crawl over to the hot stove, holding two cups, apparently knowing that the tea was just for Isaiah and myself. Taking an open pot off the stove, she began to laugh. She brought the pot to Isaiah, who began to laugh. Then she came to me. There, floating in the middle of the teapot, was a little birch canoe that one of the children must have made. With everything frozen outside, and a tight lid on the five-gallon water bucket, the tea pail was the only place to test the little craft.

Mary explained to everyone that there was a little canoe in the tea. There was a great deal of laughter as someone asked if there was a little hunter in there, too. After giving the canoe to the little craftsman, she went outside, presumably to dump the old tea.

Isaiah went to the water bucket. "Maa!" he exclaimed obviously disgusted. Verbal exclamations of surprise are cultural. "Wow!"; "Zut alors"; "Aiyee"; "Carramba"; and a myriad of others, from around the world, announce the unexpected. In Cree, "Saa!" seemed to express the surprise of sudden understanding. "Maa!" seemed to be appropriate for the unexpected. Unexpectedly, Isaiah had discovered that the water bucket was empty.

Each person, in a hunting camp, contributes to the well-being of the camp. For children, fulfilling that responsibility brings praise and pride and a sense of wanting to help. A child's failure to do a task, for whatever reason, often precipitates a dramatic display of disappointment from everyone, accompanied by an intentional display of someone having to pick up the slack. Carrying one tiny spruce bough to be woven into the floor is as important to the camp as hauling home a moose. The Crees understand that society—country or camp—is a weave of personal offerings, each important in and of itself.

The canoe-maker had been identified by the giggles from the back of the lodge when Mary looked in the tea. As luck would have it, the young man was also on water detail. The excitement of a visit from the sky had caused the matter of an empty water bucket to slip his mind. Ruben jumped to fulfill his responsibility, but it was too late. Isaiah had already picked up the bucket. Without a word, Grandpa was going to fill the water bucket. To make matters worse, he asked me to join him on the walk to the lake.

I have no doubt that Ruben heard, full well, as he watched his grandfather silently bend to go outside: *Well, I will just have to get the water myself. I have to find wood and cut it, find meat and bring it home, set traps to catch beavers to sell to the trader, deal with the manager and the minister and keep everyone happy. You would think that a grandson could bring one bucket of water from the lake every day to help out. Well, that's just the way it is going to be. I will have no one to take care of me when I am old. Ruben will be too busy building canoes. Oh well, I guess I will just have to go out in the cold and get the water myself, even if I get my moccasins wet, because I don't want our family to be embarrassed anymore in front of the minister, who can't even get a cup of tea because Ruben didn't get water this morning.* In the Cree system of discipline, silence was the strap.

I followed Isaiah through the flap.

"Ruben a good boy," he laughed.

As we walked down the frozen path, I was struck by the beauty of the place. "Your lake is beautiful."

"*Naspich tawpa*. Beautiful"

"Are there good fish in the lake?" I asked, both to make conversation and to add to my catalogue of great trout lakes.

"Eh he, trouts—big. We set nets."

Of course, that was one of the reasons that this campsite was chosen. There were good, accessible spruce boughs for the floor, good logs for the lodge, a good landing strip for planes, a good supply of fur and meat, and good fish in the lake. I had learned that Crees enjoyed trout and pickerel, but pike and other fish were used as dog food.

By this time we had reached the water hole. A trough had been cut with an axe in the ice. At the centre, a ten-inch hole had been cut with a chisel of some kind to allow the trough to fill. Isaiah passed the bucket through the trough a few times, pulling fresh water up through the hole and dumping the water on the snow. Satisfied that the water in the trough was fresh and clean, he ran the bucket through the trough one more time and turned to the camp.

I had a thought.

"Maybe I will get some string and find a hook to fish with."

Why not? This lake was probably teeming with lake trout and speckles, since only this family fished the lake, and then only every third or fourth winter.

"Good to fish, but no fish in the water hole."

"Really?" I was amazed.

There must be fish all over the lake. Maybe this particular spot did not have the right kind of bottom to attract trout, or maybe the ice was too thick and the water too shallow for trout.

"Yes, no fish in the water hole."

We walked back to the camp without saying much. Mary made tea. Everyone seemed to forget Ruben's oversight and the afternoon passed easily. I kept thinking of the trout in that lake. I did not have a rod, but the idea of a few fresh trout to take home was very appealing.

About mid-afternoon, I decided to try fishing. Rummaging through the backpack I always carried on these visits to camps, I found some light string. I asked one of Isaiah's sons if he had a hook.

"You gonna try a little ice fishing?"

"Yes, your father said there are lots of trout in the lake. I thought maybe I could catch a couple to take home."

"Oh you'll catch fish. I'll get a couple of hooks. We have some ice fishing rods you can try."

Lawrence was about my age. He was happy to help.

"Ever fly-fish?" he asked with a hopeful look.

"Yes, I love fly-fishing."

"We'll charter a plane this summer and come up here. You'll get ten-pound speckles on dry flies every cast. If we bring a canoe, we can troll for the big lakers. Let me go get the stuff. Do you want bacon or hotdogs for bait?"

"I'll try both. Get a piece of tinfoil, too. Do you have any cheese?"

His look told me that the winter camp was not the place for cheese.

Isaiah had not missed the discussion. He appeared from behind the lodge as Lawrence came back with my tackle. Laying an axe, a long-handled chisel, and a huge, tin scoop perforated with what looked like nail holes in front of me, he repeated, "No fish in the water hole."

"Ahh, my father always says that," Lawrence laughed.

"Okay, thanks, Isaiah. I'll catch trout for supper," I promised, somewhat pleased that I didn't have to ask for the equipment to cut a hole in the ice.

"Miyoshow! Good!"

Lawrence and I picked up everything gathered and given, and set off down the path to the lake. Bait and food were in my backpack. We each carried a rod that Lawrence had produced. He took the ice-cutting equipment.

Since he knew the lake, I assumed Lawrence would pick a spot for a fishing hole. To my astonishment, he began to cut a hole about twenty feet from the water hole where Isaiah had said there were no fish.

"Your father said there were no fish here," I reminded Lawrence.

"There are fish everywhere in this lake. Pick a place, cut a hole, and catch a fish."

Lawrence was already chiselling ice. Since we had only one chisel, I decided to fish while I waited for my turn.

I walked back to the water hole and decided to give it a try. The worst that could happen was that I wouldn't catch anything. When Lawrence was done with the chisel, I would cut another hole somewhere that he suggested.

Examining the rod that Lawrence had given me, I found that it had a good, open-faced spinning reel already rigged with a hook and a weight. The rod was about four feet long with a lot of flex, but somewhat thick. It had been bought for ice fishing. I took off the backpack and rummaged through things wrapped in aluminum foil until I found something that felt like bacon. Unwrapping the foil, I ripped a piece of bacon off a strip, quickly squashed the package back together and dropped it in the backpack.

I was wearing the same kind of moosehide mittens that Isaiah had dropped to his side when greeting me. It was cold enough that my knuckles were becoming stiff in just the time it took to bait my hook. I took just enough time to open the bail on my reel and drop the weighted line into the water, letting it fall to the bottom until I felt slack. The water seemed about ten feet deep. I brought the bait up off the bottom a little bit.

People often say, "But it's a *dry* cold." This is meant to be a knowledgeable comment about some area of the world where the commentator is not. Cold is cold. Somehow, the frigid temperature seemed amplified on the frozen lake despite there being no wind. But it was a dry cold.

I barely had time to get my mittens on when I felt the quick pull of a trout. Anyone that fishes a lot learns to recognize, with reasonable certainty, what is taking the line, particularly if using bait and most certainly if there is just one kind of fish in the lake. This was a trout, a large one, judging from the strength of the hit. The little rod bent and jerked. The drag, a device for allowing fish to take line rather than break it, was set too tight, preventing the fish from taking line. Not knowing the weight of line on the reel, I adjusted the drag bit by bit with the little knob on the face of the reel. This was a good trout. I yelled for Lawrence. Isaiah's prediction about fishing the water hole was forgotten in the tug of war across two mediums.

"I told you there were good fish in here," Lawrence yelled, running from where he was cutting the ice. "That's not real heavy line so don't bull him too much."

For a few moments, the struggle continued as the rod tip, bent into the hole, moved in a circular motion around the hole one way and then the other. Finally, a flash in the hole promised a huge trout, most likely a speckle, since lakers tended to head to the bottom and react to a hook much like a log.

"When the head is out of the water, grab the line as close to the fish as you can and yank him up."

Lawrence was as excited as I was. "It looks like it's pretty good."

He knew the rod, so the bend meant more to him than it did to me. I could feel the pull.

"He feels good."

There is no female personal pronoun in Cree. Someone might say, "My wife isn't here, he is at the store." So it made some sense for Lawrence to make this fish male. Why I made it male was a mystery.

Focused on the flash in the hole, I hadn't noticed Isaiah walk up. Now I caught sight of him to my left just inside my peripheral vision. He was watching the hole intently.

"I guess there are fish here after all." I laughed.

This wasn't meant to be an "I told you so" statement, but the surprised look on Isaiah's face made me think that he might have understood it that way. I didn't think about it again because my fish made a run for freedom.

I pulled back on the rod and the fish turned. Frantically, I reeled line down to the hole and then pulled back again. This steady pull was working. The fish was close. Kneeling down near the hole, I got ready to grab the line as Lawrence had suggested. I wanted this fish. I had caught lots of fish through the ice, but this was certainly the biggest.

As I knelt, I noticed that the surface was extremely hard all around the hole. This was from weeks of swishing buckets clean and dipping water. The snow twenty feet around the hole was as frozen as a skating rink. As I knelt, I lifted the rod tip as high as I could and the fish appeared. I reeled the tip down to the hole, bent over, grabbed the line close to the fish, and yanked him out of the hole.

There was a beautiful speckled trout, the biggest I had ever caught, probably over eight pounds. I hadn't noticed before, but the frozen snow was sloped away from the water hole. When I dropped the fish on the ice next to the hole, it slid behind me down the little incline. Turning to retrieve my sliding catch, I saw Isaiah watching and laughing.

"*Ka mishach,*" he laughed. "*Tapwe chi ka mokoshanaw.* Big—we feast."

Isaiah was pleased with the fish.

Lawrence had picked up my trout and was holding it with both hands. "Nice fish."

"Hey, that's the biggest trout I ever caught! Not bad, eh? How much do you think he weighs?"

"Eight or nine pounds, probably."

Isaiah had left. He was at the boulder rim now on his way back to the lodge.

"Well, let's get another!" I said, as I admired the fish.

There are tacit rules that bound most situations encountered in living with others, but sports and fishing might top the list for unspoken rules of etiquette and action. A comment or two about a good fish from everyone present is considered polite. One exclamation such as, "Yes!" or "All right!" is acceptable, with one other statement such as "Beautiful fish," or "What a fight!" from the person who caught the fish. More than that is considered gloating from the successful person and insincerity from the observers.

These brief conversations about a fish are ended rather formally with, "Let's get another one," or "Let me get my line back in the water." If an observer asks, "Whacha usin'?" it's okay to talk about bait or lure with a brief reference to the fish just landed, usually by way of explanation as to how the fish hit. Lawrence had seen everything, so he did not leave me this opening. We began to reorganize for more fishing.

Isaiah was back. He handed me a cup.

"I could use a drink."

Thanking Isaiah, I filled the cup in the centre of the hole. As I lifted it to my lips, I noticed a film over the water and a few shiny specks. I looked closer. They were fish scales. As unobtrusively as I could, with two people staring directly at me, I threw away the filmy water and dipped another cup. The same oily film and scales were there. Bending down, I scooped away the surface water with the cup and dipped again. The water was still oily.

I looked up to see Isaiah picking up the chisel at the hole Lawrence had begun.

"That's okay, Isaiah. I'll clear this hole," I called, trying to sound reassuring.

Try as I might, I could not get rid of the oily film. There seemed always to be a scale or two in the cup. Isaiah had already realized the problem and was finishing Lawrence's work cutting a water hole away from where I had caught the fish.

Laughing, he pointed to the new hole in the ice. "No fish in the water hole."

The Bear

I spent much of my youth playing basketball, but, at average height and below average athletic ability, I certainly was never a basketball player. Someone who can do plumbing home repairs is at a different technical level than a plumber. An "-er" gives the infinitive of the verb a depth of meaning implying understanding, expertise, and commitment. All my life I have known people who hunt. But I never knew a *hunter* until living with Cree native North Americans. Those who go to forest or field, on days off, for challenge or thrill or because of a taste for wild meat are hunting—or, more appropriately, *searching*. Those who live in the forest knowing they are as much a part of the land as the spruce or muskrat are hunters. Hunters love the land. They understand their place on the land, respectfully taking what they need, thankful to have another day.

The land is a place to find adventure or peace for those who hunt on days off. A friendly farm or familiar piece of rural countryside annually becomes the setting for raucous, exaggerated banter about hunts gone by, and strolls through the woods in the midst of living conditions that would be condemned by anyone who is at all health conscious. The site for this brief, seasonal escape from life can be chosen out of habit or by invitation.

But in the northern forests, the land seems to choose the hunter. Some hunters who do not have their own territory hunt by invitation from someone who needs help in a particular year. They learn the characteristics of the land, with guidance, adequately enough to survive without intimacy. Some hunters are assigned a tract of land by the government. They have the opportunity to pursue their traditional lifestyle in the forest while helping the authorities regulate the animal population. This relationship with the land is temporary and often contentious, as the hunter learns the characteristics of his territory by trial and error.

Some hunters go to the land walked by their great grandfathers, handed down through generations in anticipation of hunters yet unborn. Introduced to the land by their fathers, streams and lakes, ridges and cliffs are more than notations on a topographical map. They are signposts in a vastness. They are directions offered by the land giving help with every task. As someone who hunts leaves the comforts of home to be with friends in joyful squalor, the hunter leaves the village to be with the land.

Isaac inherited his hunting territory. Generations had cared for the same spruce bogs and crystal, blue lakes, but since creation only a few dozen people had walked the 4,000 square miles that Isaac loved. Having been introduced to the land by his grandfather, his father had shown him the characteristics of the place that would be his companion for life. He, in turn, had introduced his son to the land. Seeming to sense that Isaac was aging, the land had welcomed Joseph as a new companion. While Isaac now took care of the camp and ventured only a short distance to help gather boughs or snare rabbits, Joseph found the streams open to his crossing, showing sandbars built by spring torrents. He found ageless rocks still marking the beginning of faint, seldom-used trails. Swamps continued to provide moss for his lodge and trees willingly offered boughs and firewood. Joseph found companionship in all that surrounded him as he crossed the land. He found comfort in his father's affirmation at the end of the day.

Isaac and Joseph were not the only providers on the land seeking shelter and sustenance. Small scurriers hid in the brush or burrowed into the snow, darting here and there grabbing what the wind had blown within their reach; or digging into instinctively gathered hoards of food. Among these were mink and martin, unseen yet leaving a confused mass of tracks across the landscape in their quest to eat and hide. Rabbits ventured here and there in the underbrush, leaving a track like that of some large, loping animal, with their huge hind feet pulling forward to meet their stabilizing front paws. Mice and squirrels ventured out as daylight faded, hoping that lengthening shadows and darkness would hide their search for food.

There were those who separated themselves from potential enemies by surrounding their homes with water. The nimble muskrat, sensing danger, darted into holes in the shoreline, only to return to the lake, creating a sparkling "V" on moonlit water when all seemed safe. The beaver left his poplar dinner to retreat beneath the water to the safety of his warm, dry lodge, secure from all enemies.

Larger, stronger citizens of the forest also walked in the late evening and night. They were hunters, experts at reading signs and surviving regardless of the season. The lynx and fisher found the tiny tracks of others in the bush and followed.

The gregarious wolf lived in family groups. Pausing only to sing and hear the answer of others, they moved constantly through the night, searching for another meal. During the day, older family members lolled on sun-baked rocks or under shady branches, regaining strength for the coming evening's hunt. Pups and juveniles jumped and rolled in mock battle, sometimes spilling onto resting parents and grandparents, only to receive a warning growl or controlling nip.

Three seasons of the year, winged neighbours shared the forest with Isaac. Ducks and geese of various species stopped by his hunting territory in the spring while moving north to build a new family and in the fall while heading south for the winter. Large and small, they glided on lakes and streams or waddled on the shore, always probing for weed, grass or tiny bugs.

The errie call of the loon announced security and peace to all who heard. Suddenly, an unheard voice would tell them all to move on.

Raptors glided in warmth rising from the earth, always searching the ground for someone who had set aside caution for food. Owl, eagle and osprey were signs in the heavens for Isaac, but terror from above for many of the forest dwellers. They dove from great heights onto the smallest of unsuspecting, overly bold ground dwellers.

Foragers moved about the forest confident in their stature. Unless injured or sick, only their young had to fear visits from uninvited neighbours. The cow moose and her calf walked from bush to bush from early evening until their enormous appetites were filled, and found needed rest in a spruce bog or poplar grove. In winter, they stood in groups for warmth and protection. In warmer months, the huge bulls strode the forest in circular routes, passing the same spot every three or four days until danger or diminished food forced a change in routine.

Caribou were more timid than their huge cousins. They wandered in large groups for protection, crossing in and out of Isaac's land, foraging in the open and moving to the shelter of the forest to rest. Their magnificent antlers were adapted for survival with a huge, bone shovel acting as a sight allowing a motionless caribou to recognize stationary rock from creeping hunter.

Ceaselessly searching for food nine months of the year and retreating to a private sanctuary for the three coldest months of winter, the black bear was the most honoured resident of Isaac's territory. A medium-sized bear compared to his cousins in other parts of the world, he had an enormous appetite and an undiscriminating palate, eating almost anything that could be chewed and swallowed. Shy by nature, the bear avoided human contact whenever possible. Having no enemies when grown and healthy, the bear appeared to rule the forest.

The male could travel dozens of miles daily in his search for food and females. He was solitary except when nature drove him to find a mate, always shunning parental responsibilities with a last look backward and a sniff of the air before walking again into life. The female, after accommodating her shiftless partner, took her responsibilities seriously, from choosing a secure, warm place for the mid-winter birth, to several years of training her cub.

Isaac knew his land and the animals that lived there or passed through. He saw himself as different from each of them, but not superior. He understood that, as his son and family carried on his way of life, each of the offspring born on his land carried on the life of the parents.

I had loved the forest since boyhood days "at the lake" with my family. Always fascinated by creatures I encountered in the woods, my thoughts on animals had evolved to somewhere between Beatrix Potter and a sportsman's view of hunting for fun. I thought of an animal as a decoration in the world, to be used as needed. Although encounters, wild or domestic, were a thrill, I acknowledged no connection other than necessity and curiosity.

Isaac spent his life in the forest learning from his grandfather and father, and teaching his sons. He understood the animals on his land as he did the family members in his lodge. Always watchful of those for whom he was responsible in camp, he protected those for whom he was responsible on the land. Isaac spent much of his time hunting to provide for his family but always watching for signs of the other residents on his land, calculating numbers and food supplies. He moved lodge sites from year to year to minimize the effect his family would have on the land in one place. There were years that he did not go to his land hunting with someone else, believing the land and those who lived there needed to rest.

Each spring, Isaac moved his family from a substantially built winter lodge to a large cabin tent that could be pitched and dismantled with relative ease, enabling the entire family to travel to different parts of the territory, monitoring the land and all its inhabitants. Each year, spring camping marked the birthday of Isaac's grandson, Joseph Jr., called Joe. This year he would be sixteen.

A number of ceremonies marked significant stages of life for the Crees. Just after youngsters began to walk, the rite of passage called the "Walking Out Ceremony" marked the passage of children from their mother's side into the world, where they would learn to survive. As family and friends gathered, the children walked out of a tent carrying with them the symbols of their life's work. A girl carried a bundle of spruce boughs, a boy a small bow with arrows. Some ceremonies related to faith, others to various annual celebrations, but the most joyous gatherings celebrated the passage of time in the life of a family. The sixteenth year, as in many cultures, had been designated as a milestone in the life of a child.

Joe's birthday celebration had been anticipated for months. His family, knowing that they would be in spring camp when the day arrived, made sure that everything was prepared before they went into the bush in the fall. Isaac, knowing that I would be visiting camps in the spring, had asked me to try and be at his camp on Joe's birthday.

On the homeward leg of a trip to visit families in their hunting camps, I stopped at Isaac's camp to join Joe's birthday celebration. A chartered Cessna 185 aircraft proved most efficient for visiting a number of camps on frozen lakes. Travel by snowmobile would have been preferable, but too time-consuming. As did most families hunting any distance from the village, Isaac also had travelled to his campsite by aircraft, using dog team and canoe only to traverse his territory.

The celebration was to take place in the evening of the day I arrived. Isaac and Joseph showed me around the camp after talk of news from the village, and a service of Holy Communion. The tour began with a walk to the lakeshore not too far from the camp. The inlet for the lake was just a few hundred yards from Isaac's tent. Open water, where a small river flowed into the lake, offered an explanation of how this particular campsite had been chosen. Joe waved from a blind placed near the open water. This small circle of sticks and bark was designed to hide the hunter from geese who would be attracted to open water for rest and food on their trip north. Isaac smiled. We walked on, not wanting to disturb the hunter.

Ahead was an elevated rack made of thin spruce logs. At one end, a homemade ladder rested on the rack.

"*Taishipitagun*," Isaac pointed out as we got closer.

Just visible from the ground, bones of various sizes were scattered over the rack.

Joseph explained, "My father puts the bones of animals on this rack to honour them. We don't throw them out like garbage."

These words were a reminder of the constant struggle for life in this beautiful place. Tall, straight spruce trees, as far as the eye could see, punctuated by the occasional poplar or pine, provided contrast to the soft blue of the sky and the grey-white of spring ice, a complement of colour divinely inspired. It was hard to imagine that everything within that beauty concentrated on grasping life. Only the young, and Isaac and his family, took time to play together.

The birthday feast was a time of laughing and eating. Several families, from hunting grounds adjacent to Isaac's, had made the trip by snow machine and sled to join Joe's birthday party. A group of aunts and uncles with some young cousins had flown in from the village. All crowded into Isaac's tent, from which everything but the stove had been removed. Food, prepared in the tents of visiting families, was passed from person to person. There were goose and fish, as well as moose, beaver, partridge, and bear. The women had baked bannock, a traditional bread. Bowls of lard were passed as a substitute for butter. Other condiments were scarce, but love and friendship were in great supply. Everyone ate in family groups around tablecloths of varying descriptions spread on the spruce bough floor. Men joked about the special taste of a particular piece of meat that must have come from their camp. Children grabbed and jostled for more of everything. The women giggled quietly, watching and passing what was needed.

The feast had begun with a brief ceremony of giving back to the land. Isaac had placed a bit of tobacco and several small pieces of meat into the little wood stove. He told everyone that if they remembered to give these things to the land at each feast, they would not forget to respect the land.

Everyone got quiet as the bowls of leftover food were picked up and taken to other tents. I assumed that a birthday cake would be produced to complete the party. Joseph's wife, bending low to enter the tent, carried a roasting pan containing a large piece of meat. She placed the pan in front of Isaac. In the pan was a bear's head. Somewhat taken aback by the head, I tried to focus on Isaac as he spoke. Joseph translated for my benefit.

"The bear is the strongest and wisest animal in the bush," Isaac began. "He walks the land and uses whatever he needs, but never destroys the land. He knows that we are here and that we respect the land."

After a short pause, Isaac continued, "The bear does not own the land and neither do we. We use the land and keep it for others."

Several of the men were nodding in agreement. Even the children, who paused in their pushing, seemed to understand the seriousness of Isaac's words.

Isaac went on. "Joe is a good hunter. He has learned from his father. Someday the land will be his to use. It is Joe's birthday."

Everyone clapped and whistled. Children near Joe slapped him on the back. Joseph brought out a package.

Someone yelled, "Look at it! It's a rifle!"

"Open it, Joe. It might be a new shotgun."

The response from a knowing, young voice was immediate: "It's too short."

Joe opened the package and held up a new Winchester 30-30. He happily thanked everyone. Presents appeared from everywhere.

As the yelling and cheering began to die down, Isaac reminded everyone that the feast was not over. I was still waiting for cake. He took the pan with the bear's head and passed it to Joe. Joe cut a piece of meat off the head and passed it to his father.

Knowing that I would be wondering what was going on, Joseph explained: "When we have a bear feast, we eat a piece of meat from the bear's head so that we can be wise and strong like the bear."

Every adult male in the tent cut a piece of meat from the head—including me. I ate my piece with trepidation, but discovered that it tasted the same as any other piece of bear meat. Eventually a cake was produced. The requisite sixteen candles were blown out, and the cheering started again.

As the visitors went to their own tents, Joseph's wife offered everyone remaining a cup of tea. The conversation turned to the day's goose hunt and Joe's new rifle. Joseph translated when I was unable to understand some part of the conversation.

Through Joseph, I said that the bear meat was my first.

"*Chi miyayiten a?* Did you like it?" Isaac asked.

"*Eh, heh, weekashin!*" I replied. "It was delicious. I hunted bear back home, but I never got one," I informed everyone, having no idea why.

Isaac looked at me and explained, "The bear would not let himself be hunted by you."

Perhaps the relaxed mood after a long day of travel and fresh air had moved me to the point of indiscretion. Perhaps I was a bit insulted by the idea that I could not successfully hunt a bear. For whatever reason, I jokingly asked Isaac a question that had been on my mind since his talk about the bear. Joseph translated.

"If the bear is the wisest of the animals, why was it in the pot?"

Joseph gave a surprised laugh and translated. Isaac was admiring Joe's birthday rifle. He had been working the lever and gently releasing the hammer to check the action. Without looking up from what he was doing, Isaac answered the question in the casual manner of someone who knows exactly what he thinks.

"The bear let himself be killed so we could live."

He sighted the rifle at an imaginary target, and family life carried on.

About the Author

The Rev. Dr. James Collins was raised in a suburb of Pittsburgh, Pennsylvania. All of his post-secondary education was completed in the Boston area, where he graduated from Gordon-Conwell Theological Seminary and The Episcopal Divinity School. In 1974, James travelled to the Diocese of Moosonee, in northern Ontario, to become the Curate at St. Thomas Church, Moose Factory Island. He served as the rector of two native parishes, diocesan Program Officer, and Dean, before leaving the diocese in 1993 to move to the Diocese of Algoma. In Algoma, James served as the rector of Trinity Church, Parry Sound, and Archdeacon. In 1997, James left the North for California, where he began to work with the developmentally disabled population. He is presently licensed in the Episcopal Diocese of El Camino Real and working as a district manager for an agency that serves developmentally disabled people of all ages.

James is married with a blended family of five boys and a girl; they range in age from eighteen to thirty. His wife encouraged him to share his stories with those outside the family. Gratified to learn how much she enjoyed descriptions of events from his past, he nevertheless suspected an ulterior motive. He might have been right. Concentrating on putting events on paper distracted James, even if only for a short while each day, from constantly regaling the family with tales of the North.